Exploring Everyday Math

Ideas for Students, Teachers, and Parents

Maja Apelman and Julie King

HEINEMANN
Portsmouth, NH

Heinemann
A division of Reed Publishing (USA) Inc.
361 Hanover Street Portsmouth, NH 03801-3912
Offices and agents throughout the world

We would like to thank the children whose work appears in this
book, and the parents who have given their permission to include
that material. Every effort has been made to contact the copyright
holders for permission to reprint borrowed material where
necessary. We regret any oversights that may have occurred and
would be happy to rectify them in future printings of this work.

Some of the ideas in this book have been expressed previously in a
booklet entitled *Pizzas, Pennies, and Pumpkin Seeds,* © 1989 by the
Colorado Department of Education, and are reused here with
permission. That booklet may be purchased by contacting Virginia
Plunkett at the Colorado Department of Education, 201 East Colfax
Avenue, Denver, CO 80203.

Acknowledgments for photographs, illustrations, and previously
published material are on pages vii–viii.

Library of Congress Cataloging-in-Publication Data
Apelman, Maja.
     Exploring everyday math : ideas for students, teachers, and
parents / Maja Apelman, Julie King.
          p.   cm.
     Includes bibliographical references.
     ISBN 0-435-08341-4 (acid-free)
     1. Mathematics.   I. King, Julie, 1934–   . II. Title.
QA39.2.A63   1993
372.7′044–dc20   93-8737
                                                             CIP

Designed by Janet Patterson
Cover photograph by William Kellogg
Printed in the United States of America on acid-free paper
97 96 95 94 93 EB 10 9 8 7 6 5 4 3 2 1

To some extent, everybody is a mathematician and does mathematics consciously. To buy at the market, to measure a strip of wallpaper, or to decorate a ceramic pot with a regular pattern is doing mathematics. School mathematics must endow all students with a realization that doing mathematics is a common human activity. Having numerous and varied experiences allows students to trust their own mathematical thinking.

National Council of Teachers of Mathematics

Contents

Acknowledgments

Many people have contributed to the creation of this book. We wish to give them credit and express our appreciation.

First, we want to thank the teachers who read parts of the manuscript, gave us valuable feedback, tried some everyday math activities in their classrooms, and provided us with samples of their students' work. They include, in New England: Michelle Menegaz, 2nd grade, Academy School, Brattleboro, VT; Mary Morrissette, 2nd grade, Westmoreland School, NH; Sandi Pagniucci, 2nd grade, Hartland Elementary School, VT; Denise Sargent, 5th grade, Chesterfield School, NH; and in Colorado: Roberta Mantione, K–1st grade, University Hill School, Boulder; Lisa Johnson, 1st–2nd grade, University Hill School, Boulder; Polly Donald, 2nd–3rd grade, University Hill School, Boulder; Larry Orobona, 3rd grade, Mesa School, Boulder; Suzanne Steward-Johnson, 4th grade, Mesa School, Boulder; Craig Yaeger, 5th grade, Whittier School, Boulder; Caroline Cutler, 1st grade, Lafayette School, Lafayette; Sally Grahn, Elem. Math Specialist, Graland School, Denver; Marge Bender, 5th grade, Stanley B.P.S., Denver.

Next we wish to thank all the children whose writing and drawings greatly enrich the pages of our book. We were pleased that they responded so enthusiastically to the activities.

The illustrations of Lauren Bassing, Andre Cotto, Billy Covington, and Larry Orobona enhance and clarify the text. We thank them for sharing their talents with us.

Fifth grader Grace Larson spent much time filling out all the charts in the text. We thank Grace and her mother Laura for their interest and for helping to bring these charts to life.

Three generations of the Kellogg family were involved with this book: Elizabeth Kellogg gave us permission to use many of her wonderful pictures of children at work in classrooms; her eight-year-old grandson Kristoffer and his father Karl volunteered to do some baking for a possible cover photograph, which was taken by grandpa Will. Thank you all for your help, your interest, and your enthusiasm.

At Heinemann, we worked with two editors—Toby Gordon and Alan Huisman. Toby, the acquisitions editor, showed us how to turn a booklet written for parents into a book addressed to teachers. She helped us to see things from another point of view while validating our own educational philosophy. Toby was patient, encouraging, and supportive—the ideal person to start us out on the long road from manuscript to published book. We greatly appreciated her help. Halfway along that road, Alan Huisman, the production editor, took over. The process of production was new to us: there were many steps along the way and many decisions to be made. Alan was always available to answer our questions. He gave us options, sought our input, and made the whole process an interesting and pleasant experience. We liked working with Alan and enjoyed his good humor.

Finally, each of us wishes to acknowledge the influence of a special person who has made a significant contribution to our mathematical education: Lore Rasmussen, with whom Julie worked for twelve years in the Learning Center's Project in Philadelphia, and David Hawkins, with whom Maja worked for many years at the Mountain View Center in Boulder, Colorado. We treasure the opportunity we had to learn from these creative and committed teachers how to think about mathematics in new and exciting ways.

Thanks to the following for permission to reprint previously published material:

Page 78: Figure 5–4 © Lands' End, Inc. Reprinted Courtesy of Lands' End Catalog.

Pages 176–177: Figures 10–2 and 10–3 reprinted with the permission of the copyright owner, U S West Direct, Publishers of the White and Yellow Pages.

Page 178: Figure 10–4 © AT&T's Customer Information Center. Used with permission.

Pages 205–6: Road signs and explanations are based on the Colorado Drivers' Manuals, 1981 and 1992.

Pages 29, 76, and 97: Photographs by Elizabeth Kellog, from *Pizzas, Pennies and Pumpkin Seeds.* Used with permission of the Colorado Department of Education.

Pages 63 and 80: Figures 4–6 and 5–6. Drawings by Billy Covington, from *Pizzas, Pennies and Pumpkin Seeds.* Used with permission of the Colorado Department of Education.

Pages 87 and 209: Figures 6–2 and 12–3. Drawings by Andre Cotto, from *Pizzas, Pennies and Pumpkin Seeds.* Used with permission of the Colorado Department of Education.

Additional credits:

Pages 60, 79, 162, and 202: Figures 4–5, 5–5, 9–3, and 12–1. Drawings by Larry Orobona.

Pages 132, 197, and 203: Figures 7–17, 11–6, and 12–2. Drawings by Lauren Bassing.

Page 192: Figure 11–3. Drawings by Julie King.

Pages 26, 33, 39, 98, 136, and 145. Photographs by Elizabeth Kellogg.

Pages 92, 124, 207, and 210. Photographs by Maja Apelman.

Pages 5, 6, and 151. Photographs by Julie King.

Page 199. Photographs by Marge Bender.

Introduction

This book has two themes. The first is "everyday math"—the mathematics that touches our lives as we attend to our daily tasks—at school, at home, at work, and at play. Everyday math surrounds us wherever we live and offers rich opportunities for a wide range of mathematical activities. Bringing everyday math into the classroom addresses the problem of isolation, referred to by John Dewey as early as 1900:

> From the standpoint of the child, the great waste in the school comes from his inability to utilize the experiences he gets outside the school in any complete and free way within the school itself; while, on the other hand, he is unable to apply in daily life what he is learning in school. That is the isolation of the school—its isolation from life. (75)

When math activities center around experiences from children's lives, the mathematics may be new, but its context is familiar. Children are able to use what they know or have learned outside of school, and they can apply their school learning at home.

The second theme of the book is parent involvement. Parents know a great deal of math—they use it constantly in their daily lives. We want to make parents more aware of the many opportunities for mathematical learning in their environment and to encourage them to trust their mathematical knowledge and share this knowledge with their children.

Everyday math is an ideal way to make this connection. Most of the math activities in this book can be done at home as well as at school. Parents are important participants; their contributions are essential to the success of this approach. When there is a true partnership between home and school, everyone involved benefits.

Problem Solving and Mathematics in Schools

In the past, teachers and textbooks typically dealt with skills first, applications later. Children encountered everyday math in the classroom mainly in word problems, after the skills necessary to solve those problems had been taught. The primary goal was for students to acquire arithmetic skills; although everyone acknowledged that the reason for learning these skills was to apply them, many assumed that once the skills were in place children would automatically be able to use them to deal with everyday situations.

That view is gradually changing. There is renewed interest in learning from experience. At the same time, calculators have enlarged the scope of problem solving children are capable of before they have mastered complex computational skills. Problem solving is now regarded as one of the main goals in mathematics teaching, and math educators recognize that becoming a good problem solver requires much more than the mechanical skills needed to calculate an answer. Students need to be able to interpret questions, make conjectures, organize and interpret information, recognize patterns, draw analogies, and reason logically. These skills and the ability to orchestrate them are developed through experience. Problem solving is not just an end product, it is part of the learning process.

Recommendations for Change

When the National Council of Teachers of Mathematics published its *Curriculum and Evaluation Standards for School Mathematics* in 1989, problem solving, communicating, reasoning, and making connections headed the list of priorities. Forty other professional associations—educational, mathematical, scientific, and technical—endorsed or supported these recommendations. Embedded in the *Standards* is the idea that "'knowing' mathematics is 'doing' mathematics. A person gathers, discovers, or creates knowledge in the course of some activity having a purpose. This active process is different from mastering concepts and procedures" (7). The National Research Council, in *Everybody Counts* (1989), takes a similar stance. Everyday math is therefore beginning to be accepted as a legitimate part of elementary school mathematics.

Parent Participation

Parent participation has also received a great deal of attention in recent years. Most schools offer parents a number of opportunities to become involved with their children's education: parents can attend school conferences and meetings, serve as classroom volunteers, chaperon class trips, or become members of parent advisory groups and school improvement teams. This book offers another way for parents to take part in their children's education: the learning activities we introduce here make family experiences—everyday math—an integral part of ongoing classroom life.

Parent Mathematicians

Many parents don't feel comfortable with math, or they assume it takes special expertise to teach it. Remarks like "I never was any good at math" or "How could I teach math? I can't even balance my checkbook!" are common. However, even the parents who feel this way use mathematics all the time. They hand out lunch money, cut sandwiches into quarters, calculate how much paint or wallpaper they need to buy, estimate how much a trip will cost, read and interpret graphs, talk about the probability of rain, and decide that it's time to fill the gas tank. Some of them knit, piece quilts, measure wood for cutting, and use metric tools to work on their cars. The list goes on and on.

Many adults also feel they aren't doing things *the right way*, that they aren't really using mathematics, because their approaches, even though they work, are not the methods they learned in school. There are in fact many ways to do mathematics, and more than one can be right. People who devise their own strategies for finding answers to mathematical questions, far from being mathematically incompetent, are often excellent independent problem solvers. They are using mathematics creatively.

Eugene Maier (1977) used the term "folk math" and defined it as "the math folks do":

> Folk math is the way people handle the math-related problems arising in everyday life. It consists of a wide and probably infinite variety of problem-solving strategies and computation techniques that people use. . . . School math and folk math range over much the same topics. But folk mathematicians do mathematics with methods different from those commonly involved in school math. . . . School

math should provide children the opportunity to deal with the mathematics in their own environments in the same way proficient folk mathematicians do. (84–85)

The mathematical problems parents solve are real and immediate and have consequences for themselves and their families. What valuable experience this could be for children if parents would only recognize and share their mathematical knowledge! Parents need to be encouraged to talk about their daily activities with their children; parents and children need to think about problems and explore solutions together.

Partners in Learning

If parents share the mathematics they do, bringing their children gently into the process, children will learn some of their math by watching and trying, the way they learn to thread a needle or hit a nail. Mathematics encountered in this way will be interesting and useful. In many homes, language skills are shared and learned naturally and informally. Parents read bedtime stories, point out words on cereal boxes and road signs, write simple notes to their children, and help them write letters to relatives. Most parents also feel quite comfortable teaching their children to count and recognize simple shapes. They count all kinds of things aloud and wait patiently while their children try it themselves. They point out circles and squares and guide small hands in putting puzzle pieces in place. But most parents stop this process when it comes to arithmetic, not realizing that if they were to share some of their more advanced problem solving, their children would continue to learn from them.

The activities in this book are designed to make family experiences part of the mathematics curriculum. We suggest activities that teachers initiate in school and the children then bring home, where parents can contribute their knowledge and expertise. The results from this "home work" are incorporated back into classroom work, becoming a necessary and important part of school math projects.

A Classroom Example

An example may make this clear. Rosemary Agoglia's primary class of six- to eight-year-olds at The Common School in Amherst, Massachusetts, was engaged in a thematic study of the early settlers of the

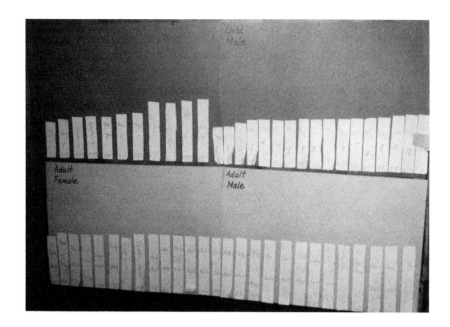

Bar graph showing the heights of children in a primary class, as well as the heights of their siblings and adult family members.

United States. They were especially curious about the *Mayflower*. What did it look like? Who was on board? Why did these passengers want to come to the United States? What was the voyage like? The students decided to make a picture of the ship. There was a large bulletin board in their classroom, and they needed to make their picture fit the bulletin board.

Since this class had previously mapped their classroom, measuring it in feet and drawing it to scale on one-inch graph paper (one inch representing one foot), the children suggested doing the same thing with the ship. Their teacher would draw the ship, using the real dimensions and working from a picture. They would draw and cut out the people to go on the ship. This presented a problem, however. They had a passenger list that named the adults and children on board but gave no heights. How would they know how tall to make people using the one-inch-equals-one-foot scale?

Their teacher suggested that the children ask their parents to help them measure the members of their families. If they wrote down these measurements, along with the ages of those who were not yet adults, they would have the heights of real people of a variety of ages to go by. The children did this. Using the measurements they brought from home, they cut strips of paper to represent the heights of family members on the one-inch-to-one-foot scale. These were mounted, forming a long bar graph, with the names and ages of those they had measured written below the strips (see photo).

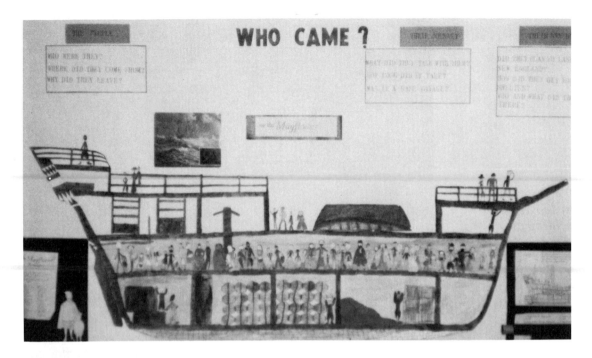

A depiction of passengers on the Mayflower. *Passengers' heights were modeled after the real people the children had measured.*

The children then chose individual passengers to draw. Since the passenger list did not specify the ages of children, they made these up. To decide how tall to make their passengers, the children modeled them on people of similar age and gender from the graph, sometimes members of their own family. The resulting collection of passengers (see photo) has the proportions of a group of real people.

There were many benefits to be derived from this project, for both the children and their parents. The children had a chance to learn more about ratio, proportion, measurement, and scale in the context of a project they really cared about. They were able to see a relationship between this and the mapping project they had done, and to make connections between math and history. They could see that mathematics is not only necessary and useful, but also that it is a way of describing a group of people—a way different from words or pictures but equally effective.

Parents were able to share their measuring skills and had a chance to communicate with their children about mathematics. Their involvement made them more aware of what was happening in the classroom. Family statistics became an integral part of a classroom project because the teacher was aware of what parents have to offer and recognized how important their contribution could be. The children's need and enthusiasm inspired their parents to participate.

How to Begin

The activities in this book are ways to get started. Trying them will help teachers involve parents in everyday math. These activities can of course be modified to fit individual teaching styles, the circumstances in which teachers work, and the culture of the community. Part 2 provides supporting material on children's learning and on explaining the everyday math program to parents.

Teachers who want to weave everyday mathematics into ongoing activities in the classroom should try not to make the at-home portions too time-consuming. It's best to choose family assignments that can be carried out in the process of daily activities or that are centered around matters of common interest to parents and children. Our hope is that teachers will use these everyday math activities in their classrooms, thus involving parents as enthusiastic and respected teaching partners.

PART I

Getting Started

1
How This Book Is Organized

Curriculum Chart

The curriculum chart at the end of this chapter directs you to activities appropriate for specific mathematical topics. The left column of the chart lists the mathematical topics in sequential order—from easy to advanced—the way these topics might appear in a math curriculum guide. (The main heading "Measurement," for instance, comprises the subheadings "Length," "Area," "Volume," "Liquid Volume," "Weight," "Temperature," and "Time.") The activities in Part 3 that address these mathematical topics are listed, by grade level, in the three remaining columns.

For instance: If you are teaching third grade and want to find an activity involving division, look up "Division" in the topic column. (It's on page 16, under "Whole Number Operations.") Next, go to the column headed "Grades 2 through 4" to find appropriate activities and the pages where they're discussed. (Division activities appropriate for the third grade are "Computing Unit Prices" from Chapter 6, "Pizza Mathematics" from Chapter 8, "Understanding Interest" from Chapter 10, and "Planning Trips" from Chapter 12.) The activity headings in the curriculum chart are listed in chapter order and correspond with the activities as listed in the chapter overviews.

Chapter Overviews

Each activity chapter begins with a chapter overview that lists the various activities included in the chapter. These activities are presented sequentially, starting with math activities for younger children and progressing to more advanced projects for the upper elementary grades.

Under each activity, further headings tell you which parts the children will be doing at school and which at home. For instance: If the third-grade teacher looking for division activities wants a quick idea of what children will be doing in "Pizza Mathematics," she can turn to the overview of Chapter 8, "Eating Out," and find out that the students will compute the areas of different-sized pizzas, make a "favorite pizza" survey with their families, and then calculate the best buys in their neighborhood pizza parlors.

The activities in each chapter are connected only by its theme. Each school–home–back-in-school project stands on its own. Start with the chapters and topics that interest you and that offer the most appropriate activities for your students. You can also look for activities that you can relate to other subjects like art, science, or social studies, or you can search for activities that would add a math component to a curriculum theme you have chosen for your class.

"How Children Learn Math"

Use this chapter, which begins on page 25, as a reference to help you reassure parents who may have questions about your math curriculum.

The first part of the chapter, "Early Mathematics," deals with the beginnings of math: sorting, classifying, matching, learning to count, and learning to measure. These discussions may help you explain the importance of early math activities to parents.

The second part of the chapter, "Mathematics in School," discusses recent changes in the elementary math curriculum and explains why certain topics are given such importance. The topics covered are:

- Creating and searching for patterns.
- Measuring with nonstandard units.
- Emphasizing problem solving.
- Using calculators.
- Learning about statistics and probability.
- Introducing geometry.
- Feeling comfortable with estimation.

Again, you can use these sections to help parents understand which aspects of math are being strongly emphasized today.

Feel free to copy any part of this chapter to send home in a newsletter or to give to individual parents who may have questions about the way the children are being taught.

Everyday Math Activities

There are nine chapters in Part 3 and they can be used in any order. The first two chapters, "Family History" and "Personal Statistics," deal with the children and with their families. The next three chapters, "Supermarket Shopping," "In the Kitchen," and "Eating Out," are about familiar activities parents and children often do together. "Money Management" is in a category by itself: a quick glance at the overview shows that considerable ground is covered, from recognizing coins and making change to managing a bank account and learning about interest. "Telephone Math" and "Taking Care of the Mail" show how much mathematical content there is in these common daily happenings. "Cars and Travel" takes you a bit further afield, offering a large number of car-related math activities.

Letters to Parents

The eight sample "Letters to Parents" in the text (and repeated in the Appendix) will give you some ideas on how to communicate with and involve parents. You can use these letters as they are, alter them slightly, or write your own versions. The letters inform parents of classroom activities, ask them to contribute materials, and make suggestions on how parents can support school learning at home. You can also include or attach relevant information from Chapter 2. (See our letter on matching in the supermarket, for example.) We hope these samples will prompt you to send many more letters home to parents.

Book Lists

A few chapters include a short list of favorite children's books related to specific topics. You will find counting books in "Counting in the Supermarket"; books on shape in "Shapes Everywhere"; and books on scale in "Geometry in a Restaurant Kitchen." More excellent children's books on these and many of the other topics in the book can be found in Gailey (1993), Whitin and Wilde (1993), and Griffiths and Clyne (1991). Try to enrich your everyday math activities with books from your school and/or public library. A collection of related books can help get students interested in your projects. Books can also extend students' knowledge and motivate them to do further research.

CURRICULUM CHART
ACTIVITIES COORDINATED WITH CURRiCULUM

TOPIC	ACTIVITY		
	Kindergarten through Grade 2	Grades 2 through 4	Grades 4 through 6
EARLY MATHEMATICS Classifying	Shapes Everywhere, p. 114 Becoming a Price-Conscious Consumer, p. 166 Behind the Scenes at the Post Office, p. 189 Road Sign Geometry, p. 204	A Kitchen Number Search, p. 109 Shapes Everywhere, p. 114 Phone Book Classification, p. 181 Behind the Scenes at the Post Office, p. 189 Categorizing and Surveying Mail, p. 193 Road Sign Geometry, p. 204	A Kitchen Number Search, p. 109 Becoming a Price-Conscious Consumer, p. 166 Behind the Scenes at the Post Office, p. 189 Categorizing and Surveying Mail, p. 193 Road Sign Geometry, p.204
One-to-One Correspondence	Matching in the Kitchen, p. 106 Matching in the Supermarket, p. 85		
Sequence	A Long Time Ago, p. 49 Behind the Scenes at the Post Office, p. 189	A Time Line of Your Life, p. 51 How Long Does It Take for a Letter to Be Delivered? p. 186 Behind the Scenes at the Post Office, p. 189	A Time Line of Your Life, p. 51 Behind the Scenes at the Post Office, p. 189
Patterns	Great-Grandparents, p. 62 Phone Number Patterns, p. 172	Great-Grandparents, p. 62 Phone Number Patterns, p. 172 Area Code Patterns, p. 174 The Numbers on an Envelope, p. 185	Great-Grandparents, p. 62 Phone Number Patterns, p. 172 Area Code Patterns, p. 174
NUMBERS & NUMERALS Counting by Rote	Counting in the Kitchen, p. 108		
Counting Objects	Describing Activities with Numbers, p. 73 Counting in the Supermarket, p. 88 Counting in the Kitchen, p. 108 Taking Traffic Counts, p. 201	Describing Activities with Numbers, p. 73	Describing Activities with Numbers, p. 73
Number Meaning	Becoming Aware of Personal Numbers, p. 67 A Kitchen Number Search, p. 109	Becoming Aware of Personal Numbers, p. 67 A Kitchen Number Search, p. 109	Becoming Aware of Personal Numbers, p. 67

TOPIC	ACTIVITY		
	Kindergarten through Grade 2	Grades 2 through 4	Grades 4 through 6
Reading and Writing Numerals	Becoming Aware of Personal Numbers, p. 67 A Kitchen Number Search, p. 109 Menus and Bills, p.146 Learning About Phone Numbers, p. 171 The Numbers on an Envelope, p. 185	Becoming Aware of Personal Numbers, p. 67 A Kitchen Number Search, p. 109 Area Code Patterns, p. 174	
Number Lines	A Time Line of Your Life, p. 51	A Time Line of Your Life, p. 51	A Time Line of Your Life, p. 51
WHOLE NUMBER OPERATIONS **Addition**	Counting Change, p. 157 Making Change, p. 160	Great-Grandparents, p. 62 Taking One's Own Measure, p. 69 Menus and Bills, p. 146 Making Change, p. 160 Saving for Purchases, p. 162 Managing a Bank Account, p. 164 A Classroom Post Office, p. 190 Categorizing and Surveying Mail, p. 193	Great-Grandparents, p. 62 Taking One's Own Measure, p. 69 Menus and Bills, p. 146 Saving for Purchases, p. 162 Managing a Bank Account, p. 164 Understanding Interest, p. 167 A Classroom Post Office, p. 190 Categorizing and Surveying Mail, p. 193
Subtraction	A Long Time Ago, p. 49 A Time Line of Your Life, p. 51 Then and Now–Differences, p. 55	A Long Time Ago, p. 49 A Time Line of Your Life, p. 51 Then and Now–Averages and Graphs, p. 57 Making Change, p. 160 Saving for Purchases, p. 162 Managing a Bank Account, p. 164 Becoming a Price-Conscious Consumer, p. 166	A Time Line of Your Life, p. 51 Saving for Purchases, p. 162 Managing a Bank Account, p. 164 Becoming a Price-Conscious Consumer, p. 166 The Family Car, p. 211

TOPIC	ACTIVITY		
	Kindergarten through Grade 2	Grades 2 through 4	Grades 4 through 6
Multiplication		Great-Grandparents, p. 62 Decribing Activities with Numbers, p. 73 Multiplication Stories, p. 116 Multiplication on a Larger Scale, p. 120 Twice as Much Cake, p. 132 Planning Trips, p. 215	A Time Line of Your Life, p. 51 Great-Grandparents, p. 62 Decribing Activities with Numbers, p. 73 Multiplication on a Larger Scale, p. 120 Twice as Much Cake, p. 132 Playing with Numbers, p. 152 Phone Book Estimation, p. 180 Planning Trips, p. 215
Powers		Great-Grandparents, p. 62 Milk Cartons and Powers of Two, p. 131	Great-Grandparents, p. 62 Milk Cartons and Powers of Two, p. 131
Division		Computing Unit Prices, p. 102 Pizza Mathematics, p. 148 Understanding Interest, p. 167 Planning Trips, p. 215	A Time Line of Your Life, p. 51 Then and Now–Fractions and Line Graphs, p. 58 Computing Unit Prices, p. 102 Comparing Capacities of Beverage Containers, p. 141 Understanding Interest, p. 167 The Family Car, p. 211 Planning Trips, p. 215
RATIONAL NUMBERS **Fractions—Meaning**	What Is One-Half? p. 122	What Is One Half? p. 122 Pizza Mathematics, p. 148	Then and Now–Fractions and Line Graphs, p. 58 What Is One Half? p. 122 Pizza Mathematics, p. 148 Yellow Page Statistics, p. 181 Planning Trips, p. 215

TOPIC	ACTIVITY		
	Kindergarten through Grade 2	Grades 2 through 4	Grades 4 through 6
Fraction Operations		Seeing Fractions in Action, p. 125 Twice as Much Cake, p. 132 Pizza Mathematics, p. 148	Seeing Fractions in Action, p. 125 Twice as Much Cake, p. 132 Pizza Mathematics, p. 148 Categorizing and Surveying Mail, p. 193
Decimals—Meaning		Computing Unit Prices, p. 102 Menus and Bills, p. 146 Saving for Purchases, p. 162	Computing Unit Prices, p. 102 Categorizing and Surveying Mail, p. 193 The Family Car, p. 211 Planning Trips, p. 215
Decimal Operations		Menus and Bills, p. 146 Saving for Purchases, p. 162 Managing a Bank Account, p. 164	Menus and Bills, p. 146 Saving for Purchases, p. 162 Managing a Bank Account, p. 164 Becoming a Price-Conscious Consumer, p. 166 The Family Car, p. 211 Planning a Trip, p. 215
Percent—Meaning			Gauging Growth, p. 74
Finding Percent of			Menus and Bills, p. 146 Saving for Purchases, p. 162 Understanding Interest, p. 167 Categorizing and Surveying Mail, p. 193
Ratio			Yellow Page Statistics, p. 181
Scale	How Are Supermarkets Organized? p. 87 Geometry in a Restaurant Kitchen, p. 144	A Time Line of Your Life, p. 51 How Are Supermarkets Organized? p. 87 Geometry in a Restaurant Kitchen, p. 144 Scale, p. 210	A Time Line of Your Life, p. 51 Road Maps and Symbols, p. 208 Scale, p. 210

TOPIC	ACTIVITY			
	Kindergarten through Grade 2	Grades 2 through 4	Grades 4 through 6	
RATE		Gauging Growth, p. 74 Computing Unit Prices, p. 102 Pizza Mathematics, p. 148 Planning Trips, p. 215	Gauging Growth, p. 74 Computing Unit Prices, p. 102 Comparing Capacities of Beverage Containers, p. 141 Pizza Mathematics, p. 148 Managing a Bank Account, p. 164 Understanding Interest, p. 167 The Family Car, p. 211 Planning Trips, p. 215	

MONEY	Learning About Coins, p. 155
	Counting Change, p. 157
	Making Change, p. 160
	Becoming a Price-Conscious
	  Consumer, p. 166
		Menus and Bills, p. 146
		Pizza Mathematics, p. 148
		Making Change, p. 160
		Saving for Purchases, p. 162
		Managing a Bank Account, p. 164
		Becoming a Price-Conscious
		  Consumer, p. 166
		A Classroom Post Office, p. 190
			Computing Unit Prices, p. 102
			Menus and Bills, p. 146
			Pizza Mathematics, p. 148
			Saving for Purchases, p. 162
			Managing a Bank Account, p. 164
			Becoming a Price-Conscious
			  Consumer, p. 166
			Understanding Interest, p. 167
			A Classroom Post Office, p. 190	

ESTIMATION		How Much Does This Bag of
		  Potatoes Weigh? p. 96
		Multiplication on a Larger
		  Scale, p. 120
		How Much Does This Cup
		  Hold? p. 135
		Menus and Bills, p. 146
		Planning Trips, p. 215
			How Much Does This Bag of
			  Potatoes Weigh? p. 96
			Multiplication on a Larger
			  Scale, p. 120
			How Much Does This Cup
			  Hold? p. 135
			Menus and Bills, p. 146
			Yellow Page Statistics, p. 181
			Planning Trips, p. 215	

TOPIC	ACTIVITY		
	Kindergarten through Grade 2	Grades 2 through 4	Grades 4 through 6
GEOMETRY **Spatial Sense**	Matching in the Supermarket, p. 85 Shapes in the Supermarket, p. 89 Understanding Volume, p. 195 Road Sign Geometry, p. 204	How Are Supermarkets Organized? p. 87 Shapes in the Supermarket, p. 90 Twice as Much Cake, p. 132 Understanding Volume, p. 195 Road Sign Geometry, p. 204	Twice as Much Cake, p. 132 Understanding Volume, p. 195 Surface Area and Volume of Boxes, p. 197 Road Sign Geometry, p. 204
Identifying Shapes	Shapes in the Supermarket, p. 90 Shapes Everywhere, p. 114 Road Sign Geometry, p. 204	Shapes in the Supermarket, p. 90 Shapes Everywhere, p. 114 Road Sign Geometry, p. 204	Road Sign Geometry, p. 204
Properties of Shapes	Shapes Everywhere, p. 114 Shapes in the Supermarket, p. 90	Shapes Everywhere, p. 114 Shapes in the Supermarket, p. 90	
Similarity	Geometry in a Restaurant Kitchen, p. 144	Geometry in a Restaurant Kitchen, p. 144 Scale, p. 210	Scale, p. 210
MEASUREMENT **Length**	A Time Line of Your Life, p. 51 Describing Activities with Numbers, p. 73	A Time Line of Your Life, p. 51 Taking One's Own Measure, p. 69 Describing Activities with Numbers, p. 73 Gauging Growth, p. 74 Road Maps and Symbols, p. 208 Scale, p. 210 Planning Trips, p. 215	A Time Line of Your Life, p. 51 Taking One's Own Measure, p. 69 Describing Activities with Numbers, p. 73 Gauging Growth, p. 74 Road Maps and Symbols, p. 208 Scale, p. 210 The Family Car, p. 211 Planning Trips, p. 215
Area		Pizza Mathematics, p. 148 Scale, p. 210	Pizza Mathematics, p. 148 Area Code Patterns, p. 174 Surface Area and Volume of Boxes, p. 197 Scale, p. 210

TOPIC	ACTIVITY		
	Kindergarten through Grade 2	Grades 2 through 4	Grades 4 through 6
Volume	Understanding Volume, p. 195	Twice as Much Cake, p. 132 Understanding Volume, p. 195	Computing Unit Prices, p. 102 Twice as Much Cake, p. 132 Understanding Volume, p. 195 Surface Area and Volume of Boxes, p. 197
Liquid Volume	Comparing Capacities of Beverage Containers, p. 141	Milk Cartons and Powers of Two, p. 131 Twice as Much Cake, p. 132 How Much Does This Cup Hold? p. 135 Comparing Capacities of Beverage Containers, p. 141	Milk Cartons and Powers of Two, p. 131 Twice as Much Cake, p. 132 How Much Does This Cup Hold? p. 135 Comparing Capacities of Beverage Containers, p. 141 The Family Car, p. 211
Weight	How Much Does This Bag of Potatoes Weigh? p. 96 Behind the Scenes at the Post Office, p. 189	Gauging Growth, p. 74 How Much Does This Bag of Potatoes Weigh? p. 96 Behind the Scenes at the Post Office, p. 189 A Classroom Post Office, p. 190 Categorizing and Surveying Mail, p. 193	Gauging Growth, p. 74 How Much Does This Bag of Potatoes Weigh? p. 96 Behind the Scenes at the Post Office, p. 189 A Classroom Post Office, p. 190 Categorizing and Surveying Mail, p. 193
Temperature	A Kitchen Number Search, p. 109	A Kitchen Number Search, p. 109 Twice as Much Cake, p. 132	Twice as Much Cake, p. 132

TOPIC	ACTIVITY		
	Kindergarten through Grade 2	Grades 2 through 4	Grades 4 through 6
Time	A Long Time Ago, p. 49 Then and Now–Differences, p. 55 Becoming Aware of Personal Numbers, p. 67 Describing Activities with Numbers, p. 73	A Long Time Ago, p. 49 Then and Now–Averages and Graphs, p. 57 Family Reunions, p. 60 Becoming Aware of Personal Numbers, p. 67 Describing Activities with Numbers, p. 73 Where Do Bananas Come From? p. 100 Multiplication on a Larger Scale, p. 120 Becoming a Price-Conscious Consumer, p. 166 How Long Does It Take for a Letter to Be Delivered? p. 186	Family Reunions, p. 60 Describing Activities with Numbers, p. 73 Where Do Bananas Come From? p. 100 Multiplication on a Larger Scale, p. 120 Becoming a Price-Conscious Consumer, p. 166 The Family Car, p. 211 Planning Trips, p. 215
STATISTICS **Sampling**	Taking Traffic Counts, p. 201	Taking Traffic Counts, p. 201	Categorizing and Surveying Mail, p. 193
Data Collection and Recording	Then and Now–Differences, p. 55 Taking Traffic Counts, p. 201	Then and Now–Averages and Graphs, p. 57 Gauging Growth, p. 74 Pizza Mathematics, p. 148 Area Code Patterns, p. 174 How Long Does It Take for a Letter to Be Delivered? p. 186 Taking Traffic Counts, p. 201	Then and Now–Fractions and Line Graphs, p. 58 Gauging Growth, p. 74 Pizza Mathematics, p. 148 Playing with Numbers, p. 152 Area Code Patterns, p. 174 The Family Car, p. 211
Organizing Data	Taking Traffic Counts, p. 201	Pizza Mathematics, p. 148 How Long Does It Take for a Letter to Be Delivered? p. 186 Taking Traffic Counts, p. 201	Pizza Mathematics, p. 148

TOPIC	ACTIVITY		
	Kindergarten through Grade 2	**Grades 2 through 4**	**Grades 4 through 6**
Bar Graphs	A Time Line of Your Life, p. 51 Taking Traffic Counts, p. 201	A Time Line of Your Life, p. 51 Then and Now–Averages and Graphs, p. 57 How Long Does It Take for a Letter to Be Delivered? p. 186 Categorizing and Surveying Mail, p. 193 Taking Traffic Counts, p. 201	A Time Line of Your Life, p. 51
Line Graphs			Then and Now–Fractions and Line Graphs, p. 58 Gauging Growth, p. 74
Pie Charts			Categorizing and Surveying Mail, p. 193
Coordinates		Road Maps and Symbols, p. 208	Road Maps and Symbols, p. 208
Mean, Median, Mode	Becoming Aware of Personal Numbers, p. 67	Then and Now–Averages and Graphs, p. 57 Family Reunions, p. 60 Becoming Aware of Personal Numbers, p. 67 Describing Activities with Numbers, p. 73	A Time Line of Your Life, p. 51 Family Reunions, p. 60 Describing Activities with Numbers, p. 73
Predicting		Then and Now–Averages and Graphs, p. 57	Then and Now–Fractions and Line Graphs, p. 58 Yellow Page Statistics, p. 181

PART II

Involving Parents

2
How Children Learn Math

Parents have a wealth of practical knowledge about their children. This knowledge can become the basis of a beneficial educational partnership between parents and teachers. In conferences, phone conversations, meetings, or workshops, you can discuss with parents their children's learning style and pace and share with them the ways in which the children are developing. Such an understanding will help parents to play a larger role in their children's mathematical education and to become familiar with the purposes of school activities.

This chapter explores some of the ways you can help parents better understand how children learn mathematics both in and out of school.

Early Mathematics

Before they enter school, children learn to do a large number of things without the benefit of any formal teaching. They learn to walk, to talk, to relate in different ways to family members and friends, to invent games and play imaginatively with all sorts of objects and toys. They learn to find their way around home and neighborhood, to master household routines, and to help with the work in kitchen, home, and yard. We don't know exactly *how* children learn all these things but we do know *why* they learn them: children have a tremendously strong drive to explore the world around them and to master the tasks of daily living.

Parents watch, guide, and encourage their children. They help them learn how to count, and teach them the names of geometric shapes. These things are clearly recognized as mathematical. What parents may not realize is that many other things they do with their children also prepare them to become good mathematicians.

SORTING, CLASSIFYING, AND MATCHING
Early mathematics includes more than counting and learning the names of shapes. Mathematics begins with such simple things as sorting, classifying, and matching.

Mathematics involves logical thinking, which in turn depends on one's ability to classify things. We classify numbers as odd or even, positive or negative, whole numbers or fractions. We classify shapes as rectangles, circles, triangles, and so on.

Sorting involves classifying. In order to sort, you must be able to perceive likenesses and differences. Young children need time and experience before they can identify how things are alike and how they are different and before they can tell you by what kinds of likenesses they have sorted something. The more experiences children have in sorting simple things like buttons, crayons, or silverware by size, color, shape, or some other attribute they may think of, the more adept they will become at noticing and describing a variety of ways in which things can be the same or different.

The classification games children play in kindergarten and first grade give them excellent practice in logical thinking and in stating in their own words by what attributes they are sorting a mixed collection of things. They especially enjoy classifying themselves: children with dark or blonde hair; children with long or short hair; children wearing sneakers, sandals, or laced shoes; children wearing pants, skirts, or dresses; children wearing shirts with stripes and children wearing

First-grade boys sort aggregate after a field trip.

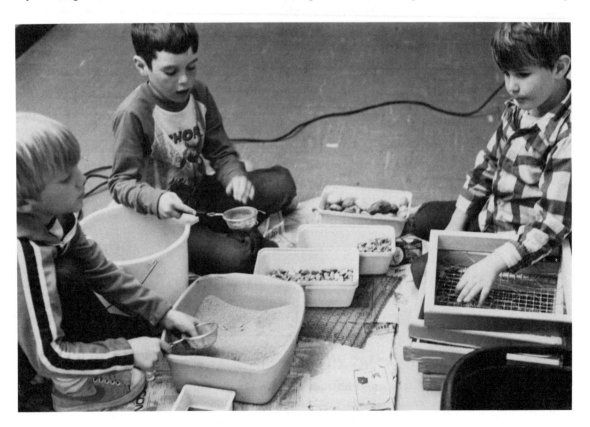

shirts with no stripes. More complicated games may involve identifying those who are *not* wearing sneakers, who are wearing sneakers *and* have blue eyes, or who are *either* wearing sandals *or* something green. These sorting activities with things or people prepare children for seeing similarities and differences in numbers and shapes. Logic is the key word here, and logical thinking is key to mathematical problem solving.

Children let us know that they have classified a group of objects by naming them. When a child says "Car!" and points to a car we know that child has successfully identified at least some of the characteristics of this set of vehicles. If she later exclaims "Car!" while pointing to a truck, we know that her "car" category isn't exactly the same as ours; it needs refining.

Matching involves making associations or seeing relationships between things. When we match two things we have in mind a reason why they belong together. Two shoes or two mittens match if they are mirror images of each other. Shirts match pants if their colors harmonize. Of particular importance is one-to-one matching. One and only one button goes in each buttonhole. You give one and only one favor to each person at a party. Children practice matching one-to-one when they fit pegs into a pounding board or use a separate paintbrush for each color of paint on an easel.

Successful counting depends partly on knowing how to match things one-to-one. In counting, children must be able to match exactly one number word with each object being counted. (See "Matching in the Kitchen" in Chapter 7.)

COUNTING

Learning to count involves more than being able to recite number words. Full understanding of counting develops gradually over a long period of time.

Learning to count takes a long time and is a more complex process than most people realize. To understand this, it is helpful to look at counting from the child's point of view.

Imagine that you are learning to count. You match the number words you have memorized to some raisins. As you touch the first raisin, you say one, as you touch the second raisin, you say two, and so on, which may seem a mysterious process. You go through the identical motions as you touch the objects to be counted, yet each time you make that motion you have to say a different word. And you have to learn another very strange thing: when you say two the preceding one is part of the two, and when you say three the preceding one and two are part of the three. If you are counting six raisins, you must understand that raisins number one through five are included in the number six. The position of raisin number six in the total collection of raisins indicates that five raisins have already been counted. If you eat raisin number five, raisin number six becomes raisin number five.

Many young children think at first that number words are names for the objects being counted, just as Carol and Kenny are names of people. Carol and Kenny are always called by the same name, regardless of whether they are in a small group, in a long line, or by themselves. A bunch of colored blocks can be used to make all kinds of patterns using different numbers of blocks. Yet the same red block may be number two in one arrangement, number five in another, and number eleven in a row. Children have to learn that the number words are not names for these blocks: they simply tell us *how many* blocks there are in a particular collection.

Some parents will have observed the stages in which their own children have developed the ability to count:

- Children hear number words being used (one, two, three, and so on) and repeat them the way they repeat all words they hear.
- Soon they try to recite the number words in the sequence in which they hear them, but it takes quite some time before they can always say them in the right order. At first number words are just like nonsense syllables—children have not yet connected them with the numbers they identify.
- Finally children begin to use the number words they have memorized to count objects. Their first attempt may involve just waving a hand around over the objects while saying number words, as they have seen adults do. If they are counting cookies, they may skip some and count others twice, because they do not yet understand that each cookie may be touched or counted only one time. Eventually they realize that to count things you match each number word with exactly one of the objects you are counting and that touching the objects helps. It takes time before children are able to do this accurately with large numbers of objects.

To understand counting fully, children must also learn that:

1. The order of counting does not matter. If the objects are lined up, you can start at either end or in the middle, as long as you count every object only once.
2. The appearance of the objects to be counted does not matter. Objects can be pushed together into a pile or spread out, arranged into rows or circles or scattered randomly. If there are eight objects

Learning to count.

to be counted, there will always be eight objects, no matter how much you move them around.

3. Groups of very different things can be counted. Children generally start out counting groups of identical objects. Later they learn that collections of objects having nothing to do with each other can also be counted. What do the wheels of a car have in common with a group made up of an elephant, a banana, a marble, and an aspen tree? There are four things in each group.

Learning to count correctly is a process that can take a long time. Encourage parents to enjoy their children's progress, however slow it may seem to them, and to accept their emerging ability to count the way they accepted their ability to walk and to talk. It doesn't pay to be in a hurry. With lots of practice and encouragement, children will learn to count with confidence and enjoyment. (See "Counting in Rhythm" and "Counting Objects" in Chapter 7.)

CONSERVATION

A young child's perception of number and size is very different from ours and depends very much on shape and arrangement. An understanding that the number of a collection does not change when things are rearranged, or that the amount of a substance like clay remains the same even when its shape changes, develops naturally. Explanations are of no use if children are not yet ready for this idea.

The principle that the number or amount remains the same when things are rearranged or reshaped is called *conservation*. Parents may be unfamiliar with Piaget's conservation experiments. They may be surprised to learn that when they spread out a group of objects, a young child thinks there are more, or that the child believes that when juice is poured into a wider glass, there is less juice because it doesn't come up as high. Adults are so sure of their point of view, it never occurs to most that children perceive things quite differently. When parents do realize children's different way of thinking, they often suppose that a simple explanation will enable the child to see "the truth." In fact, a child sees things in an adult way only when he or she is ready.

Parents need to be assured that this *will* happen and that there is no point in pushing. Instead, they can help by giving their children many opportunities to reshape substances and rearrange objects in their play—to push, pull, steer, handle, mold, stack, fit, arrange, etc. It's just as important for parents to talk with their children about size and position, using all the words by which these qualities are described: more, less, not as much, big, little, bigger, smaller, large, tall, long, short, narrow, wide, far, near, above, below, in front of, behind, and many more. (See the Helpful Hint about invariance in Chapter 7.)

INFORMAL ARITHMETIC

Many children develop their own methods of doing simple addition and subtraction—perhaps even multiplication and division—to solve practical problems before they learn number facts in school. The basis of this knowledge is counting.

Playing with numbers is something children do spontaneously, for their own enjoyment. They count just for the fun of it. They pose problems and solve them. By the time they start school they have developed their own informal practical arithmetic. They share cookies (division), decide how many more forks they need to put on the dinner table, and figure out how many toy cars are lost. You might hear a four-year-old say, "And if you get three more then we'll have the same amount!" or "I'll give two to you, and two to you, and two to me. That's six." Children who can do this are not necessarily ready for formal arithmetic. The problem 3 + 5 on a worksheet may be meaningless to the same child who can easily determine that the three pennies you just gave her, added to the five she already has, come to eight cents.

When they see that their children are able to solve simple practical problems, parents may be tempted to move on to written addition and subtraction. Try to help parents understand that learning to use formal symbols for the ideas in one's head takes time and that it is more important for young children to become confident in their practical arithmetic than to rush prematurely into written work. Using symbols too early often interferes with children's natural progress and subverts their enjoyment of mathematics.

EARLY MEASUREMENT

Measurement begins with comparing and ordering. Young children need lots of experience before they can decide whether one quantity is larger than another or arrange things in order of size.

By building with blocks, pouring water from one container to another, and participating in dramatic play, young children develop ideas of larger and smaller, longer and shorter, more and less, heavier and lighter, and so on. Many children's stories and toys are related to these concepts—*Goldilocks and the Three Bears*, stacking toys, and nesting wooden dolls are a few examples.

At first children have a difficult time comparing the lengths of two objects because they look at only one end, ignoring the other. Two new crayons, side by side, may be seen as having two different lengths if their ends are not lined up. Asked to line up three straws from the smallest to the largest, a child, looking only at the right end, might do this:

In addition, young children may think that the length of an object changes if it is turned—that a person is taller standing up, for instance, than lying down. Eventually they are able to compare lengths by lining things up, compare weights by using their hands or a balance, and compare capacities by pouring.

In true measurement, we not only compare the sizes of two things, we ask *how many* of one it takes to be as long as or as much as the other. Seeing how many small cups will fill a pitcher and counting how many blocks it takes to make a track across the rug or how many marbles will balance a block are all experiences in measurement. At an early stage, rulers, scales, and tape measures are useful only as play items, for imitating what adults do with them.

Mathematics in School

It's not surprising that many parents have trouble recognizing the current elementary school math curriculum. Most of us have forgotten a great deal about how we learned math, perhaps because we were unaware at the time that we *were* learning it. Flash cards, worksheets, and drill may be what parents remember best. They may not think of the more practical experiences, like making a paper design or trying to figure out how many minutes there are until recess, as mathematical activities.

In addition, mathematics in elementary schools has changed in the last twenty years. The availability of calculators and computers has called into question the amount of time spent on perfecting one's ability to carry out complicated arithmetic procedures. Educators have been rethinking what is important for people to know about mathematics. High on the list of recommended skills are problem solving, reasoning, communicating, recognizing patterns, and making connections. Learning arithmetic and measurement is still considered important, but geometry, statistics, probability, and estimation are now also part of the early math curriculum. The primary focus of mathematics education is problem solving.

This section summarizes a number of the new topics and emphases that parents as well as teachers need to know about. Many of the mathematical activities you will be sending home are based on these topics. While parents may enjoy the activities, they may wonder whether this is really what children should be doing in elementary school math. You can assure them that it is.

PATTERN

Pattern is at the heart of mathematics. Learning to perceive and create patterns in general gives children a great head start in recognizing and using the countless patterns that exist in numbers and in shapes.

G. H. Hardy (1945), a great mathematician of the early twentieth century, said, "A mathematician, like a painter or a poet, is a maker of patterns" (84). Pattern is everywhere: in art, music, and language; in architecture and design; in the natural and the man-made worlds; in the rhythm of our daily lives as well as in our behavior; and, of course, in numbers and shapes. We use, record, search for, and create patterns. We find pleasure in their regularity and rely on their predictability.

In many kindergarten and first-grade classrooms, children are encouraged to make, look for, and listen to patterns. They create patterns in color and shape using all kinds of materials: they string beads, make long rows of different-shaped wooden blocks, or design patterns with crayons, yarn, or different types of seeds. They learn about musical patterns through rhythmic clapping. Children also learn how the same pattern can appear in different forms: they may clap the rhythm _ . . _ . . _ . .; string a necklace of red-blue-blue-red-blue-blue-red-blue-blue beads; look for the same stress-nonstress pattern in the syllables of children's names, like Jennifer, Annabelle, or Ferdinand; or line up in a pattern of tall-short-short-tall-short-short-tall-short-short children. Later they will explore two- and three-dimensional patterns.

First graders create patterns using geometric shapes.

Searching for patterns can be very absorbing. As children progress in their mathematical studies, patterns assume an ever more important role. In work with fractions and in algebra, geometry, and calculus, an understanding of the relationships between numbers is crucial. Children who learn to see patterns in numbers in their early school work and develop what is known as "number sense" are much more likely to enjoy mathematics and to be successful in their studies. Discovering number patterns can be deeply satisfying. It often gives children confidence because pattern reveals some of the underlying structure of mathematics and shows that numbers behave in a predictable way.

FORMAL MEASUREMENT

Measuring with ordinary objects as units prepares the way for understanding what measurement is all about. To measure length, area, volume, weight, or angles we choose an object to serve as a unit and then count the number of those units it takes to make something as long (or as extensive in some other way) as the object being measured. To measure time or temperature we also need to have a starting point.

Just as children can learn to "count" by memorizing the number words without really knowing what they mean, so they can learn to "measure" by using the numbers on rulers or scales without understanding what measurement is really about. When we count objects, we are dealing with separate, individual things. We count to find out how many things there are. When we measure, we are dealing with a continuous quantity, like a length, that cannot be counted. Measurement does involve counting, but it is units of measure we count—standard units, like inches, or nonstandard units, like toothpicks—rather than objects. A set of things cannot have two different *numbers* of objects, but an object can have many different *measurements* depending on with which unit we choose to measure.

Beginning measurement activities most often use nonstandard units: straws, toothpicks, pieces of rope cut to equal lengths, whole pencils or crayons, parts of the body, etc., for length; tiles, squares on a grid, or sheets of paper for area; sugar cubes, wooden blocks, or small cups of rice for volume; washers, pennies, or marbles for weight. Using objects like these helps children focus on the process of measuring rather than on learning to read the markings on rulers or scales.

Given a one-foot ruler, an adult can measure a six-foot table by marking the end of the ruler and sliding it along. Children who are learning to measure cannot do this at first. They actually need to line up enough units to match the object being measured and then count the units. To measure area, they cover a surface; to gauge the volume of a solid object, they build one like it with cubes; to gauge the volume of a large container, they fill it up using a small one; to measure weight, they balance an object with smaller units of weight. Later they will learn to use the measuring instruments and formulas that are, in fact, short cuts for this process.

Children who learn measurement this way find metric measurement no more complicated than measurement with inches, pounds, and degrees Fahrenheit. It simply employs different units. In that respect they are probably well ahead of their parents, who may feel ill at ease with metric measurement. In addition they come to some important realizations about measurement that are very helpful in solving practical problems: the larger the unit, for example, the smaller the measure. Being aware of this principle makes it possible to reason out whether to multiply or divide when converting from inches to feet or pounds to ounces.

PROBLEM SOLVING

Memorizing facts, learning arithmetical procedures, and getting right answers are important, but should not be emphasized at the expense of understanding, enjoyment, and self-confidence. The primary aim of mathematics in the elementary school curriculum is to develop the ability to solve problems.

Mathematics would not have maintained its place in the curriculum if its purpose were simply to train children to memorize facts and follow sets of rules. What we really want children to learn is how to deal with the situations they will encounter in life, make humane and informed decisions, appreciate the beauty of the world around them, and think creatively. These abilities involve thinking about questions for which there are no ready answers, and that is exactly what a problem is—a question one does not immediately know how to answer. A problem is a question or situation about which one has to think.

In our day-to-day lives, we are confronted with problems all the time. "I've got a problem with my car. The alternator light keeps coming on but my mechanic can't find the reason." "We have a problem scheduling our family vacation. Johnny is playing in a tennis meet and doesn't want to miss it." "We found the perfect house but can't buy it till we sell our old one." How do we solve such problems? There are no easy answers, no formulas we can apply, no quick ways to dispose of them. We have to *think* about such problems, look at them from different points of view, and compare alternatives. We solve problems all the time, using many different approaches. Problem solving skills are *thinking* skills, in mathematics as well as in the rest of life.

Many people, when they first hear the word "problems" mentioned in connection with mathematics, may be thinking of the "story problems" or "word problems" that used to be found in most math textbooks. They have unpleasant memories about these paragraphs that were supposed to help you apply the math you had learned in school to the real world. Unfortunately a majority of these story problems had nothing to do with the real world of children, but were simply vehicles for practicing the skill introduced on the previous page. Often all the problems on a page were meant to be solved in the same way. They didn't challenge children's thinking and therefore weren't real problems. Old textbook story problems, writes Eugene Maier (1977), describe "no place I have ever been or wanted to be" (84).

Today we encourage children to solve problems in a variety of ways. We help them develop a repertoire of effective problem-solving strategies, among them:

- Using real objects to represent the problem.
- Acting out problems.
- Drawing pictures or diagrams.
- Looking for patterns that may give clues.
- Replacing large numbers in the problem with smaller ones.
- Making a list or table to organize the information.
- Trying to remember a similar problem solved before.
- Using trial and error (also called "guess and check").
- Finding missing information by looking in a book or asking someone.
- Cooperating with other people to solve the problem.

To adults brought up in the old tradition, in which talking was not allowed and there was only one "right" way to solve every problem, some of these strategies may sound like cheating, particularly using trial and error and cooperating with other people. Yet trial and error is one of the first strategies adults themselves try when faced with a problem they aren't sure how to solve, and many jobs involve working in cooperative problem-solving situations. Mathematicians themselves use such methods to solve problems.

In many of the newer math programs, problem solving is part of the process of learning facts and procedures, not just an afterthought. Facts and procedures retain their importance as problem-solving tools but they are not ends in themselves. There is a new emphasis on learning in the context of real or at least realistic situations. This makes parents a vitally important resource.

Parents don't have to make up story problems: the family setting naturally gives rise to many real mathematical problems. At the supermarket parents can hand their children the change and the cash receipt and ask whether the change is correct. They can ask what the backpack on sale for twenty percent off will actually cost, with tax, or how many days they should stop the newspaper delivery if they will be gone from July 3 through July 21. We need to let parents know how important it is for them to invite their children to help think through such questions. If children know their thoughts and ideas are valued even when they are not correct, they will not be afraid to tackle new problems. Problem solving then becomes a challenge rather than a chore.

CALCULATORS

Calculators can be creative tools for exploring mathematical ideas. When used as aids to problem solving, they can free children to concentrate on strategy.

The predominant objection to using calculators in the elementary school is that if children use calculators they will not learn arithmetic. Such concern is understandable, but calculators used appropriately—to explore number patterns and relationships or to relieve children of the tedium of computations so they can focus on the process—can actually enable children to learn arithmetic faster and with more enjoyment.

The availability of calculators does not mean that children don't need to have a good command of the facts of arithmetic. It is impossible to use a calculator effectively if you aren't proficient enough at mental arithmetic to be able to estimate the size of the answer. Children who are adept at mental arithmetic will know when they have pushed a wrong button and will not accept a nonsensical answer just because it appears in the calculator's window. They may also discover that there are times when the mind is more efficient than the calculator.

Using calculators also allows children to experience the excitement of real problem solving at a time when their knowledge of arithmetic is still rather limited. Many children are intrigued with large numbers, for instance, love to write them down, but cannot yet add or multiply them. If they know what addition or multiplication is, however, they can use the calculator to solve problems involving large numbers. Even children who can handle the calculations gain by being allowed to use a calculator. Finding out how many times your heart beats in a year isn't much fun if you have to labor over it with paper and pencil.

There is another good reason for parents to let their children use calculators: it puts everyone on a par while solving problems. Trying to answer interesting questions can become a cooperative project. When a child realizes that she can do computations as fast as her mother can, she may become more adventurous in looking for strategies and trying them out.

Calculators are here to stay. They are used by almost everyone, for personal as well as for business computations. Parents use calculators themselves. As they become less and less expensive, calculators may become as common a tool as pencil and paper. It makes sense to explore the new possibilities they open up and to make the most of them.

STATISTICS AND PROBABILITY

Statistics and probability have gained a place in elementary school mathematics not only because they are increasingly a part of our information-oriented society but also because they allow children to raise and answer questions about things of interest in their own environments.

Advertisements, sports scoreboards, weather reports, and newscasts bombard us with statistical information. Children need to know something about how to interpret this information if they are later to draw their own conclusions as knowledgeable citizens and consumers. Fortunately, the process of gathering, organizing, and analyzing information is one they can carry out themselves at a very early age. Kindergartners, for example, make graphs from real objects. They stack blocks to see whether there are more red, more blue, or more yellow ones. Elementary school students survey other students to find out what kinds of ice cream are most likely to sell at the school fair. Older children learn to organize information using tables, charts, and graphs of various kinds, then use them to generate questions as well as to come up with answers and make decisions.

Statistics lead quickly to probability—determining the likelihood that something will happen in the future by looking at the experiences of the past. Children in the middle grades encounter probability in games, while those in the upper grades begin to use their numerical skills to describe probability more precisely. When the weather forecaster says there is a sixty percent chance of rain, today's upper elementary students know they may be wearing boots and raincoats!

GEOMETRY

Children need to have many chances to handle and manipulate geometric shapes before they are ready for formal geometry. The

development of spatial sense is an important facet of elementary mathematics.

Children who play with blocks and puzzles and move and manipulate objects in their play are developing the ability to visualize how two- and three-dimensional objects look, behave, and fit together. This spatial sense will be a great asset in their later study of geometry.

We live in a world replete with shapes and patterns, both natural and man-made. A generation ago the study of these things was reserved for formal geometry, and available only to those who had passed through the gates of algebra. In the late nineteenth century, though, children were exploring geometry in kindergartens modeled on the ideas of Friedrich Fröbel (Leeb-Lundberg 1970). In many schools today, children are again beginning to explore geometric patterns, tessellations (tiling patterns), symmetry, three-dimensional

A first-grade boy uses unit blocks to build an enclosure.

shapes, geometric patterns in nature, and numerical patterns in geometry. Adults who quilt, weave, do carpentry, or engage in a number of other creative occupations will have a special appreciation for this aspect of school mathematics. They may be wonderful resources for your class. Parents who struggled through high school geometry may gain a new perspective of what the subject is all about if you can share with them some of the geometric activities your children do in the classroom.

ESTIMATION

Estimation is a legitimate mathematical activity and has a place in the elementary school curriculum.

A large number of the calculations we do every day are estimates. Often an estimate is all we need (for example, when we want to know whether we have enough money to pay our supermarket bill), and the additional time spent on exact calculation would be wasted. Sometimes the information we need for an exact calculation is inconvenient or impossible to get (How many Americans are there at this very moment?). Sometimes we make an estimate just to be sure we're in the ballpark (when we are using a calculator, for example).

Estimation has other benefits for children who are learning mathematics. It can help them avoid careless errors in computation, and it is essential when they start learning to use a calculator. In addition, simplifying the numbers in order to estimate the answer to a word problem focuses attention on the relationships in the problem and often reveals the kind of calculation one needs to do. For example, which is a better buy, a three-pound-two-ounce box of apples for $2.44 or a one-pound-fourteen-ounce box for $1.47? Rounding off to a three-pound box for $2.40 versus a two-pound box for $1.50 creates a simpler problem: the first box costs 80¢ a pound and the second, 75¢ a pound. Not only is this estimate fairly accurate, it also points up that the way to solve the problem is to divide the cost by the amount in order to find the unit cost. The complexity of the original numbers tends to blur one's vision.

It is only recently that estimation has come out of the closet. For most of us, "That's a guess, not the exact answer, isn't it?" meant "You're wrong! You're not thinking. Wake up!" Whatever estimation techniques we use, we developed on our own. These days, techniques for estimating are actually taught, and in solving problems children are encouraged to decide for themselves when an estimate is appropriate.

3
Explaining Your Program

A Workshop for Parents

Although organizing and leading a math workshop for parents may be a new experience, remember that you don't have to be a specialist to talk to parents about their children's math program. All you need is the desire to share the kinds of activities children enjoy and to help parents see the purpose of these activities. This chapter helps you plan an introductory workshop for parents in which you can explain why you want to use everyday math in your curriculum and why the parents' involvement and participation is important to the program's success.

FORMAT

Your workshop can be either a special event or part of an open house on parents night. Choose whatever format feels comfortable. The important thing is to let parents know how they can support their children's math learning in everyday ways that don't take a lot of time. You can also reassure parents that you do not expect them to play the role of math teacher.

When you're ready to do the workshop, decide whether you will invite your students to attend. If the workshop is to be a separate meeting, send a letter home (see Figure 3–1) to let parents know that their attendance is important.

Figure 3–1.
Letter to parents announcing a math program workshop. (A reproducible master for this form letter is included in the Appendix.)

Dear Parents,

    This year I want to help your children see how mathematics is used in everyday life, so that they can learn new skills in practical, enjoyable situations. The math you use at home will be an essential part of this program. It won't take any special expertise on your part—just your willingness to share what you already know and do every day.

    Please come to a meeting that I have scheduled to give you an opportunity to find out more about our program. We will meet in Room ＿ at ＿ p.m. on ＿＿＿＿＿＿＿＿＿ .

                           Sincerely,

WHAT YOU CAN ACCOMPLISH

1. You will be able to describe your program, let parents know how they can become involved, enlist them as partners, and help them recognize the importance of their role.

2. You'll be able to help parents see how much math they use every day, alert them to the opportunities they have at home to share their mathematical knowledge, and talk with them about tasks involving mathematics for which children could take responsibility.

3. You can brainstorm lists of mathematically useful items around the house, like measuring instruments or games, and discuss the issues related to whether children should use calculators.

4. You will find out something about the parents' concerns, and you will be able to reassure them that their concerns will be taken into account.

5. You can outline the new trends in mathematics teaching discussed in the previous chapter and help parents understand how your program fits into the recommended new approaches to the elementary math curriculum.

INTRODUCTORY REMARKS

At the beginning of the workshop let the parents know why you want them to participate in your math program:

- They have a great deal of important mathematical knowledge to share.
- Children learn best from the people who most accept and respect them.
- Learning is more lasting when it takes place in the context of familiar home experiences.
- Children must see that math is not just a subject studied in school but is used constantly in everyday family life.
- The home is an ideal place in which to learn mathematics because the problems encountered there are real, not just paragraphs in textbooks.

You may also want to tell them about the major shift taking place in today's elementary mathematics curriculum. Rather than simply teaching individual arithmetic procedures, schools are moving toward helping children use their skills to become confident and competent problem solvers. Share with your parents some of the recommendations of the National Council of Teachers (1989) discussed in the previous chapter.

ACTIVITIES

A few warm-up activities will illustrate the points you have made in your introduction and serve as examples of the kinds of things parents and children may be asked to do at home. Choose two or three activities from the following list:

1. *What Mathematics Did You Use Today?* (math in the everyday world). Give everyone a blank three-by-five card on which to write something he or she has done that day that involved some math. Put the cards in a hat and have each person pull out a card and read it. You can also have everyone do this orally, listing on the chalkboard all the examples given.

2. *How Tall? How Heavy? How Hot? How Soon?* (measurement). Give parents five minutes to write down all the measuring instruments they can think of that they own or have in their homes. Compile a master list when they've finished. Don't overlook clocks, automotive instruments, utility meters, or thermometers. Most people are amazed by how many they have. A measuring-instrument survey is an excellent family activity that can stretch out over many weeks.

3. *What's in My Pocket?* (problem solving). Ask for a volunteer to tell you the total amount of change he or she has in pocket or purse. Let the others guess what coins that person could be holding. Since there will be a number of possible solutions, this is a good example of problem solving. Repeat the activity, but this time ask the volunteer also to tell how many coins there are. Scrap paper and pencils should be handy.

4. *How Many Steps?* (estimation, graphing). Ask the parents if they remember how many steps there are on each of their home's stairways. Most of them will have to make an estimate. (If the children are also present, they and their parents can discuss and try to agree on this.) Then ask everyone to estimate how many steps they climb at home every day. Distribute vertical strips of lined paper and ask each person to color in a space for each step. Post the strips, with names beneath, to form a graph.

5. *When's Your Birthday?* (interpreting graphs). Write the names of the months in a horizontal line across the bottom of the chalkboard. Then ask the parents to come up and place a large X above the month of their birthday. After everyone has done so, ask them to study the graph and make observations about the distribution of birthdays.

Describing Your Program

The "How Many Steps?" activity is an example of the kind of project you will ask parents to become involved in. Explain in more detail how this will work. Projects will be started or set up in school. Then the children will take the problems home, where an essential part of the work is done with the aid of or in conjunction with their parents and siblings. Parents may be asked to:

- Add ideas.
- Talk about how they do something.
- Provide information.
- Discuss topics of common interest with their children.
- Supply needed objects.
- Participate in problem solving or experiments.
- Help children brainstorm.
- Encourage and help children to take on a responsibility that involves using mathematics.

The results of this "home work" are brought back to school to be used in a new learning experience: children may pool information they have found at home, analyze it, display the results, make a book, or use what they have learned as a stepping stone to understanding new concepts.

A few concrete examples of the at-school, at-home, back-in-school sequence may give parents a better understanding of the kind of work they will be expected to do. "A Time Line of Your Life" from Chapter 4, "Shapes in the Supermarket" from Chapter 6, or "Traffic Counts" from Chapter 12 are all easy to explain.

This is also an excellent time to give parents a preview of the first home/school activity you plan to do. Letting parents know about their responsibilities will give them a chance to contribute their own ideas, air their concerns, and ask any questions they may have.

Getting Started

Some parents may want to get started even before you begin the first activity in school. If so, ask them to think about the kinds of everyday mathematical tasks they do in which their children could participate. List their suggestions on the board, adding ideas from the list below if necessary. Ask parents to check off tasks they might be willing to let children take over.

Read the weather thermometer

Set a timer

Read water, electric, or gas meter

Set the thermostat

Sort the laundry

Clip food coupons

Write (not sign) a check

Measure cooking ingredients

Plan a garden

Program the VCR

Choose new clothes (within a price limit)

If children are present at the workshop, they can check off tasks they think they would be able to do if given some help. Parents and children can then compare the checked items on their lists.

At the conclusion of the workshop, ask parents to fill out a questionnaire such as the one shown in Figure 3–2.

If you and the parents enjoyed this workshop, you may want to do others from time to time. You could build them around topics from the everyday math activities in this book and have parents and children work together. Alternatively, you might want to discuss some of the topics in Chapter 2 in more depth to help parents better understand how children learn mathematics.

Figure 3–2.
Parent workshop questionnaire. (A reproducible master for this questionnaire in included in the Appendix.)

Your name _____

Your child's name _____

How do you feel about being part of a home/school math program? _____

Do you have any special suggestions for this program?

_____

_____

_____

Do you have any interests or talents that involve math and that you would be willing to share with the class? _____

If so, what are they? _____

_____

Please add any other comments or suggestions you would like to make. _____

_____

_____

_____

_____

Thank you for coming, and thanks for your help!

PART III

Everyday Math Activities

4
Family History

Every family has its unique history, and most children are fascinated with stories about their parents' childhood or their grandparents' lives. Listening to family members tell stories from the past, asking questions about what school was like then, looking at old household and kitchen artifacts if they have been saved, trying on old clothes, identifying photographs, all these activities will help children develop a better understanding of the past.

In the process of learning more about their family's past, children will have many opportunities to use the mathematics they already know. They will also be introduced to new mathematical topics. Subtraction, multiplication, number lines, exponents and exponential growth, ratio and percentages, all arise naturally in a study of family history.

A Long Time Ago

What does "a long time ago" mean to young children? They might say: "A long time ago when my daddy was a little boy" or "A long time ago when Christopher Columbus discovered America" or "A long time ago when there were dinosaurs walking around." At first, children don't differentiate well between the recent and the distant past. Historic dates are meaningless, and even a ten- or twenty-year time span may be beyond their comprehension. It will help children's understanding if you can approach the past by moving back from the present gradually, in small time segments, using familiar people and objects as concrete illustrations of what it was like "a long time ago."

IN SCHOOL: HOW MANY YEARS AGO?

Ask parents to send along a photograph of their child as a baby and to label it with the age of the child when the photo was taken. Display the pictures without names and ask the children to guess who's who. When the pictures have been identified, help each child figure out how long ago his or her photograph was taken and make a label with this information. To make this easier for young children, round off their age in the photograph to the nearest year. Then they can count backward from their current age to find out how many years ago the photograph was taken.

Include yourself in this project. Bring in some photographs taken when you were small and, if you still have some, a few toys or books that you enjoyed as a child. Tell the children how old you were when each picture was taken. If you don't mind revealing your age, tell them how old you are now and ask the class to figure out how many years ago that was—it's a good problem-solving experience. Share some recollections and let the children ask you questions as they look at the things you brought to school.

AT HOME: HOW LONG AGO?

Send a note home to parents telling them of the discussions you have had with the class about the baby pictures and let them know that their children will be asking some questions about the past at home, too. Explain that this work is an important part of your math and social studies curriculum and that the children will share the information they obtain. If parents have old photographs, encourage them to talk about "how long ago" they were taken: "Here is a picture of your big brother ten years ago at his first birthday party. . . . This is Aunt Molly all dressed up to go to kindergarten. I wonder if she remembers how she felt twenty-five years ago? . . . And here's a wedding picture of Grandma and Grandpa—that was fifty years ago!"

Ask parents, grandparents, and other family members to talk about what things were like when they were the age your students are now:

- How did they dress?
- What did they eat for breakfast?
- What kind of appliances and utensils did they have in their kitchens?
- What did their classrooms look like?
- How did they get to school?
- How much homework did they have?
- What sort of games did they play?
and so on.

BACK IN SCHOOL: SHARING "LONG AGO" FACTS FROM HOME

The children will need plenty of time to talk about the things they find out. During class discussions, you can list all the things that were true when your students' parents were children (twenty-five or thirty years ago) and when their grandparents were children (fifty or sixty years ago). These lists can be bound as books for the class, or they can be written on chart paper and displayed on the bulletin board. The children can also write "long ago" stories they heard at home, or draw and paint what they imagine things were like.

You can also organize a special "a long time ago" day and invite family members, older members of the school staff, and community members with interesting backgrounds. Display the children's work and ask the visitors to bring photographs, clothes, and other memorabilia to share with the class. Then adults can pair up with children to talk about past times.

A Time Line of Your Life: Number Lines and Graphs

Elementary school children have their own history, even if it consists of only five or ten years. On a time line, children can record important events in their lives—the birth of a sibling, a family move, or getting a puppy—as well as significant accomplishments—taking their first step, riding a bike, or being allowed to walk to school.

Making a personal time line can also introduce students to the idea of a number line. (If your students are already familiar with number lines, a time line illustrates a useful application.) Comparing their time lines with those of siblings or parents will give children an opportunity to see a graphic representation of time and to get a sense of the relative size of numbers.

IN SCHOOL: MAKING TIME LINES

For kindergartners and first graders, prepare strips of paper about five inches high and eighteen inches long, divided into three equal sections. Head (or let the children head) the sections "When I was little . . ." "When I got bigger . . ." "Now I can . . ." Ask the children to make drawings and write or dictate the text for each section. In one first-grade class, children wrote about crying and sucking their thumbs when they were little, playing in the sandbox or with their

Figure 4–1.
A first grader's
time line.

dolls when they got bigger, riding their bikes and playing ball now (see the time line in Figure 4–1 for one example). In subsequent discussions, these first graders brought up many more examples of things they could do now that they couldn't do when they were younger. Becoming aware of personal growth is one way of talking about the passage of time.

Let older children make a time line by dividing wide register tape into equal sections, one for each year of their life. Give them a three-by-five card to use in marking off equal sections five inches long, or, if they know how to measure in inches, ask them to cut off a long-enough piece before they divide it into sections. A calculator may be helpful for them to use in figuring this out. You can also let your students decide the scale everyone should use based on the amount of bulletin board or wall space available to display the time lines.

Some children may want to record birthdays on the time lines before entering events and accomplishments. Below each birthday, they can also write the year in which it occurred. For example:

1	2	3	4	5	6
1987	1988	1989	1990	1991	1992

When the sectioned tapes are ready, a group discussion may help your students get started. One child's memory of an event tends to jog other children's memories, so that more and more facts will be recalled. You can help by asking questions: Did you ever move from one town to another? Were you ever snowed in? Do you remember a special trip, like going camping, visiting grandparents, taking your first plane ride, or going to Disneyland? If children remember events and accomplishments but are not sure how old they were at the time, have them make a list to take home so that they can ask their parents. The older the children are, the more history they can record! (Figure 4–2 is a time line created by a fifth grader.)

When the time lines have been completed, let the children compare and discuss them. Then ask your students to speculate how long their siblings' time lines would be, or their parents' or grandparents' if they know these ages. Let them cut a tape for Great-Aunt Martha, who is seventy-eight, if they want to. A young child could mark off seventy-eight sections using the card—good experience in both counting and persistence. An older child could figure out how long the tape should be in feet and inches, using the scale agreed upon, then measure off that length.

AT HOME: FAMILY TIME LINES

Have the children take their time lines home to share with their families and encourage them to get their parents and siblings to make their own. The children can help figure out how long their parents' and siblings' time lines would be and offer to bring the appropriate length of tape home from school. Comparing their own time lines and those of their parents, or perhaps even their grandparents, will give children a new and vivid sense of the differences in their life spans. It may also spark discussions of significant events in family history.

Family time lines can be intensely personal and not all parents may want to share them with the class. Let them know that you understand this but that if they are willing to send in their time lines you would welcome them in the classroom.

BACK IN SCHOOL: COMPARING TIME LINES

In your classroom, clear some floor space on which children can stretch out any time lines they have brought from home. Ask whether they can tell without looking at the numbers which time line belongs to the oldest person and which to the youngest. How? Then let them look at the ages. Have they successfully identified the time lines of the oldest and youngest people? If not, perhaps all the time lines are not drawn to the same scale (using the same length to represent one year).

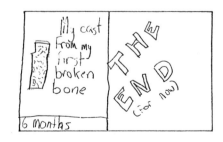

Figure 4–2.
"Amy's Life."

Mark any that use a different scale. Older children can figure out how long these would be if redrawn to the scale used in class.

Other questions you might ask are: How could you make this collection of time lines into a bar graph? (Line up the ends? Make sure they all use the same scale? Make labels?) Do we have space on our walls to display this graph? How could we make the graph smaller? (You could redraw the time lines on graph paper, using the width of one square for one year, or you could fold each time line in fourths or eighths.) Let the students come up with answers.

There are a great many fascinating numerical facts that can be derived from the time lines:

- How much older is the oldest person than the youngest? How many times as old?
- How much older than you is the oldest person in your own household? How many times as old?
- What is the median age of all the people for whom there are time lines and for all the people in your household?
- What is the average age [the mean]?
- How much older are parents, on the average, than children?

Such questions may well continue to be asked as long as the time lines are on display in your classroom.

Then and Now

Children can make many comparisons between the present and the past. Using differences, graphs, averages, ratios, and percentages will help them understand how their lives differ from those of previous generations. At the same time, they will see how these mathematical means of comparison are used. Some of the necessary information may be gathered by talking with older family members, but some of these "then and now" facts may need to be researched in books.

Differences

How often were you fed when you were a baby and how often do you eat now, including snacks?

THEN AND NOW: HOW OFTEN DID I EAT?

NOW

KIND OF MEAL	Breackfast	Snack	Lunch	Snack	Dinner	Snack
TIME	8 am	10:30 am	11:45 am	3:30 pm	5:30 pm	8 pm

I eat ___6___ times a day.

WHEN I WAS A BABY

KIND OF MEAL	Milk	Milk and Cereal	Milk	apple juice	milk and furit	Milk
TIME	6 am.	9:30 pm.	12:30 pm.	3:30 pm.	6:30 pm.	10 pm

I was fed ___6___ times a day.

Figure 4–3.
"How often did I eat?" chart. (A reproducible master for this form is included in the Appendix.)

IN SCHOOL: HOW OFTEN DO YOU EAT?

Pose this question and ask your students, as a class, to list the times at which they eat snacks and meals in school. Ask each child to expand the list to include normal snack times and mealtimes at home. When the lists are completed, let the children transfer the information to a chart like the one in Figure 4–3. They can name or illustrate the type of meal in each box.

AT HOME: WHEN YOU WERE A BABY

Ask the children, with the aid of a parent, to fill in on the chart the times at which they were fed when they were babies. If they have a baby brother or sister, they can record his or her feeding times too.

BACK IN SCHOOL: COMPARING THEN AND NOW

When the charts are returned to school ask the children to divide into three groups: those who ate more often when they were babies, those who eat more often now, and those who eat the same number of times. Ask the first two groups: How many times more often? How do you know? Let them write about what their charts show.

Averages and Graphs

How many hours in a twenty-four-hour period did you sleep when you were a baby and how many hours a day do you sleep now?

IN SCHOOL: HOW LONG DO YOU SLEEP?

Ask the children to write down the hour at which they go to sleep and the hour at which they usually wake up on school days. Then let them figure out how many hours they ordinarily sleep each night. This can be opened to group discussion if they have not done similar calculations before.

Write the number of hours for each child on the board and ask for estimates of the average. Then have the students compute it.

AT HOME: WHEN YOU WERE A BABY

Students should talk with their parents to get the information they need about their sleep habits as babies. Information about baby brothers' and sisters' sleeping habits can also be recorded (see Figure 4–4).

BACK IN SCHOOL: COMPARING AVERAGES

Have the children make bar graphs showing the numbers of hours they sleep now and slept as babies. Make one for the class average, too. Ask how many hours less the average student sleeps now. Is this more or less than half the number of hours he or she slept as a baby? Let the children answer the same questions for their own graphs. What do they think will happen as they grow older?

THEN AND NOW: HOW LONG DID I SLEEP?

Now I go to sleep at _9:30 pm_ and wake up at _7 am_ .

I sleep _9 1/2_ hours each night.

When I was a baby I slept more often.

I went to sleep at	and woke up at	I slept
7 pm	10 pm	3 hours
10:30 pm	6 am	7 1/2 hours
6:30 am	9 am	2 1/2 hours
10:00 am	12 pm	2 hours
2 pm	3:30 pm	1 1/2 hours
—	—	— hours

I slept _16 1/2_ hours each day.

Figure 4–4.
"How long did
I sleep?" chart.
(A reproducible
master for this form
is included in the
Appendix.)

Fractions and Line Graphs

How much does it cost to go to the movies today? How much did it cost when your parents and grandparents were your age?

IN SCHOOL: SURVEYING MOVIE COSTS

Survey your class to see how much different members spent for a child's admission the last time they went to the movies. Let the children find the average cost. Ask how much they think it might have cost when their parents or grandparents were young.

AT HOME: OLD-TIME MOVIE COSTS

Ask the students to survey their families, recording both the price of admission for a child and the approximate year. Older siblings can be included along with adult relatives.

BACK IN SCHOOL: TRACING TRENDS

Let students compare their findings and help them analyze these findings in various ways: What was the *average price* your parents and grandparents paid? What *fraction of today's price* was that? *How many times their price do you pay?*

The information can be pooled to make a line graph, listing the years (by fives) along the horizontal axis and the ticket prices on the vertical axis. Plot the price for each year for which a student has information and connect the points. The graph will dramatize inflation. Talk about what it shows: When were prices increasing the fastest? Why might that be? Can you tell from the graph when tickets might have cost half as much as they do now? Can you guess how much they might cost in ten years?

If students think that a graph of the price of bread, milk, or some other commodity might be similar or different, they can also explore those costs.

There are many other interesting "then and now" facts children can research with the help of their families and librarians.

- How long did it take your grandma to:
    Get home from school?
    Clean the house?
    Prepare a meal?
    Do the laundry?
- How long does it take to do these things now?
- How old were men and women when they got married fifty or a hundred years ago, and what is the average marriage age now?
- How large were families fifty or a hundred years ago, and how large is the average family now?
- How long did people live in past years, and how long can you expect to live today?
- How tall were your ancestors compared with people living now?

Once you tackle challenging questions like these, you and your students will undoubtedly think of many more.

Family Reunions: Relations

Family reunions are popular events these days. We live in a large country with a mobile population, and many of your students are probably living far from their relatives. Some children may see their grandparents only once or twice a year, and they may never have seen some of their other relatives. A large family get-together can be a very special occasion for children. Mathematically it's an opportunity to think about relations, time, and distance.

IN SCHOOL: REAL OR IMAGINED FAMILY REUNIONS

Ask your students if they have ever been to a family reunion, and have those who have had that experience share it with the rest of the class. If no one has been to one, find out what children know about family reunions: Who attends? Who would come to a reunion of *your* family? Encourage the children to talk about relatives, where they live, how often they see them, how many relatives they know, and so on.

Relationships between people have a lot in common with relations between numbers. What kinds of "people relationships" do the children know about? Some will be two-way relationships: I am your cousin, you are my cousin. Some are only one-way relationships: If I am your mother, you are not my mother. (What could you be?) Ask your students to think of other two-way and one-way relationships. You can diagram some of these, using arrows (see Figure 4–5), and encourage the children to make diagrams of others.

Figure 4–5.
Diagrams of brother/ sister and brother/ brother relationships.

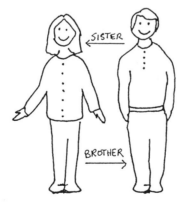 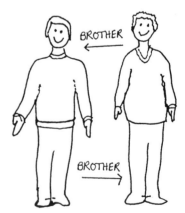

HELPFUL HINTS FOR TEACHERS

Number Relations

Later in mathematics students will identify different ways, called *relations,* of pairing up numbers with each other. One important relation is that of equality. When two numbers are equal, it is like two people being cousins: the relationship is the same both ways. A relation of inequality ("less than" or "greater than") between numbers is more like the mother-daughter or uncle-niece relation between people. Two is less than five, but five is not less than two. You can ask children if they can think of some ways numbers can be related. Numbers can't be cousins or grandmas of other numbers, but they can be "one more than" or "half as large as" other numbers.

After a discussion of family and number relations, have groups of children make lists of the relatives they know and brainstorm additional questions they would like to have answered. Some things children may ask are:

- Where would our family reunion be held?
- How many family members would come to our reunion?
- How many relatives do I know and how many have I never met?
- How far do we have to travel to get there?
- How far would our relatives have to travel to get there?

The questions can be written on tagboard for children to copy, or you can make photocopies for them to take home.

AT HOME: FAMILY FACTS

Family members can help the children do the necessary research to find the answers to their questions. They may need to write some letters to distant family members to get all the facts. Give them plenty of time to gather the necessary information.

BACK IN SCHOOL: WRITING AND ILLUSTRATING

You can now pose additional questions based on the information the children researched at home. For instance:

- What would the average traveling distance be?
- What age would the youngest person be? the oldest?
- What would the group's average age be?
- How many men, how many women, and how many children would be present?
- How many people live in the community in which they were born?
- How many times have people moved?

Students should answer these questions for their own families, using the information they gathered at home. It will be interesting for them to see how often questions are answered using mathematics.

After working out all the mathematical questions, children can now write illustrated stories about real or imaginary family reunions, using the information they brought from home. Some children may want to use family trees for their illustrations (see next section). The stories can all be bound in one volume. A page can be added at the back on which you can give averages for the whole class. For instance: The median number of relatives at our reunions was ____ . Relatives traveled an average of ____ miles to get to their reunions. Ages of family members ranged from ____ to ____ .

Great-Grandparents: Doubling and Powers of Two

Doubles of numbers seem to be facts that children learn early. "One plus one is two; two plus two is four; three plus three is six" is a familiar childhood chant. It's not a big step from here to the idea of successive doubling: "One plus one is two; two plus two is four; four plus four is eight. . . ." This process comes into play immediately when you begin exploring ancestors and family trees.

IN SCHOOL: COUNTING BRANCHES OF THE FAMILY TREE

One way to help children think about doubling is to ask them to draw pictures of four or five generations of their family (direct ancestors only). (An example is shown in Figure 4–6.) Do the first few steps—you, your parents, and your grandparents—on the chalkboard to demonstrate the form of a family tree and let the children recognize the growth pattern: each person has two parents (natural parents, not stepparents), the two parents each have two parents, which amounts

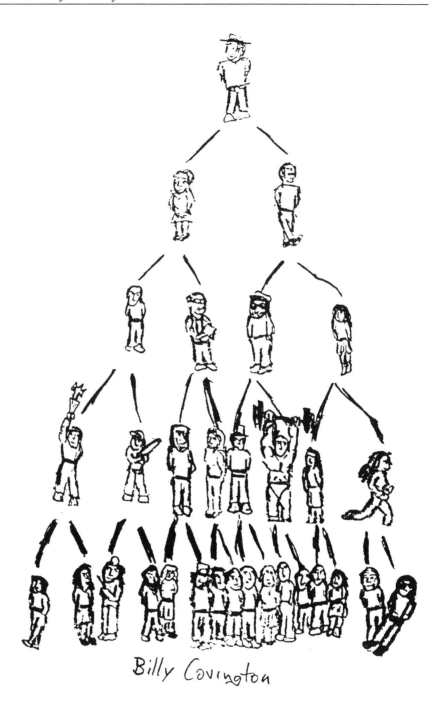

Figure 4–6.
Billy's family tree.

to four grandparents; each grandparent has two parents, and so on. How many people will each student have to draw to represent five generations?

By doubling the members of each successive generation, you quickly get to rather large numbers. There are four grandparents, eight great-grandparents, sixteen great-great-grandparents, and so on. Give your students calculators to perform these doubling computations. Some children will be satisfied with figuring out the number of people in just four or five generations, others will enjoy going further back and seeing how fast numbers grow when doubled over and over. This sort of playing with numbers and number patterns really fascinates some children. Encourage this playfulness—it is an important aspect of doing mathematics.

Introduce older children to the mathematical notation used for "powers of two": *exponents*. Make a table to show the results of doubling, starting with the number 1:

Double once	1×2	$= 2$	$2^1 = 2$
Double twice	$1 \times 2 \times 2$	$= 4$	$2^2 = 4$
Double three times	$1 \times 2 \times 2 \times 2$	$= 8$	$2^3 = 8$

Students can continue this pattern: How large would 2^{10} be? What about 2^{20}?

AT HOME: NAMING THE BRANCHES

Give the children their family trees to take home so that their parents can help them name as many of these ancestors as possible. Tell parents that the family trees are being used in studying doubling, so that only the child's direct ancestors are included in the tree made in school. Suggest that if children have stepparents, half brothers and sisters, etc., they could draw a second family tree at home that includes these relationships. Parents can help children think about how to do this.

BACK IN SCHOOL: HOW MANY ANCESTORS?

How many people would there be in a picture of you and four generations of your ancestors? The powers of two tell us how many ancestors we had in different generations: in addition to you, there are two parents, four grandparents, eight great-grandparents, and sixteen great-great-grandparents. Five generations add up to thirty-one people $(1 + 2 + 4 + 8 + 16)$; in ten generations there would be 1,023. Imagine how many people there would be if you also included brothers and sisters, cousins, and aunts and uncles! Ask your students to experiment with this, and challenge them to look for patterns in their results.

Making number lines, adding, subtracting, multiplying, doubling, measuring, graphing, dealing with scale, finding averages, thinking about relations, solving problems of time and distance, learning about exponents, all are elementary school math skills that children can develop while exploring their own and their family's history. In the process they learn that numbers can tell stories and open doors to a fascinating past.

Chapter 5   Personal Statistics

5
Personal Statistics

Almost all children are interested in facts and figures relating to themselves: How old am I? How tall am I? How many teeth have I lost? How fast can I run? are just a few of the many personal facts that can be discovered by counting or measuring. The variety of baby books on the market is a good indication that parents, too, are interested in documenting facts about their children's growth and development. Children whose parents have kept such records are fortunate in being able to recapture landmarks of their past. If few or no records exist, it is not too late to begin. Today's records will be tomorrow's personal history.

As children gain the ability to read, write, and measure, they can record their personal numbers and statistics themselves. In the following activities we suggest some ways in which personal statistics can become part of your work in the classroom. Children can make a special book in which to keep their records, adding information and accomplishments as the year progresses. As personal profiles begin to emerge from the facts contained in the books, children can decorate the covers and select suitable titles.

Becoming Aware of Personal Numbers

Numbers are part of our lives from the moment we're born. A newborn baby's length and weight are entered into the hospital's records, together with the date and time of birth. After starting our lives with these four uniquely personal numbers, we soon gain more: age, street address, zip code, telephone number, and social security number, to name just a few.

IN SCHOOL: STARTING PERSONAL NUMBER BOOKS

Ask your class what kinds of personal numbers they know about. If some of the youngest children do not know their birth dates or their house and telephone numbers, this will be a good opportunity to learn them. If they have learned to read numerals, you can help them start off their number books by writing down these numbers, along with their ages. Children who can already write numerals can do it themselves. Older children will probably come up with quite a long list of additional numbers that identify or characterize them in some way.

HELPFUL HINTS FOR TEACHERS

Numbers and Numerals

To a mathematician, numbers are ideas and numerals are the symbols for those ideas. The *number* two is something a pair of twins, your thumbs, and the headlights on a car have in common. People around the world use a variety of words and symbols to refer to this number: two, *deux, duo*, 2, II, 1 + 1, 8 − 6, and so on. Outside of this box we will use "number" to refer to both numbers and numerals, as people do in ordinary conversation. It's a good idea, though, to use "numeral" occasionally when discussing the symbols with children so that they will get accustomed to hearing the word used appropriately.

AT HOME: FINDING OUT MORE

Give the children notes to take home in which you tell the parents about the number-book project. Ask them to provide, if possible, their children's birth weight and length, the age at which they first walked, and any other personal statistics they think would be of interest. (This activity could be done in conjunction with the "Then and Now" activities in Chapter 4.)

BACK IN SCHOOL: USING THE NUMBERS

After the children enter the new information from home in their personal number books, choose one topic at a time and focus on the data the children have collected. If you choose the age at which they first walked, for example, you can write each age on a card in large print and let the children arrange these in order from youngest to oldest. Have them find the card in the middle (the *median* age).

The personal number books will also be excellent sources of data for graphing.

Taking One's Own Measure

Height and weight are perhaps the first kinds of personal measurements that occur to us, but they are by no means the only ones of importance. Buying clothing, rings, and sporting gear require people to know many other personal measurements that will be explored in this section.

IN SCHOOL: MEASURING IN PAIRS

Children can pair up to measure each other. Here are some personal measurements they can make:

- The *length of* fingers, hand (wrist to middle fingertip), arm, leg, foot, hand span and arm span (compare right and left measurements wherever applicable; are there differences?).
- The *width of* hand, eyes, nose, mouth (in repose and smiling broadly).
- The *circumference of* fingers, wrist, upper arm (with muscle both flexed and relaxed), neck, head, waist, chest, and hips.

How children make these measurements will depend on their level of understanding. Very young children can cut pieces of string the same length as whatever they are "measuring," then make a display. For example, you can ask them to cut string the same length as their eyebrows, their noses, and their smiles. With these they can make self-portraits in their books, gluing the pieces of string in the appropriate places and filling in the details with crayon or marker.

Older children can use the standard or nonstandard units of measure with which they are familiar, recording the measurements first on a worksheet and then, with care, in their books. (A class of third graders, for example, took a variety of body measurements and produced the graphs shown in Figures 5–1, 5–2, and 5–3.)

AT HOME: MEASURING THE FAMILY

The kinds of personal measurements made in school can be extended to the whole family. These measurements, which should be made by the child, can be used for projects like making string portraits of other members of the family or answering such questions as:

■ Which member of your family has the broadest smile?

■ How far can your family reach altogether?

■ Which members of your family have feet that are longer than yours and which members have shorter feet?

Make a list of questions like these and let each child choose one to investigate at home. Ask them to bring to school the measurements from which they determined their answers.

Figure 5–1.
Graph of head circumference measurements.

BACK IN SCHOOL: WRITING ABOUT MEASURING

Give the children time to write about what they did at home. Illustrations may be the clearest way to communicate the results. Display the drawings and written accounts.

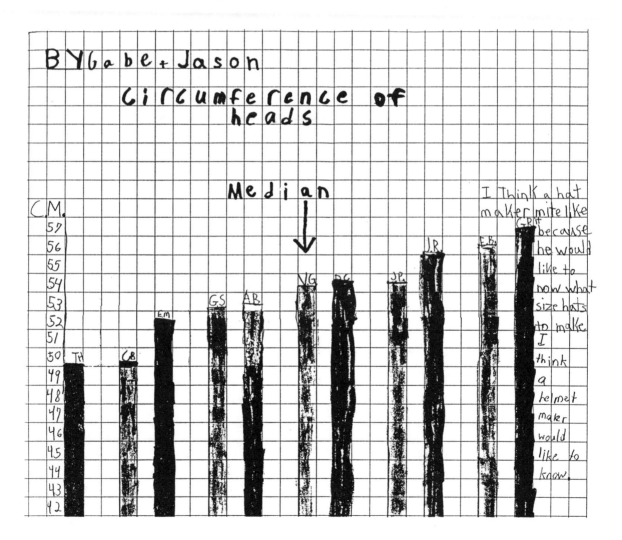

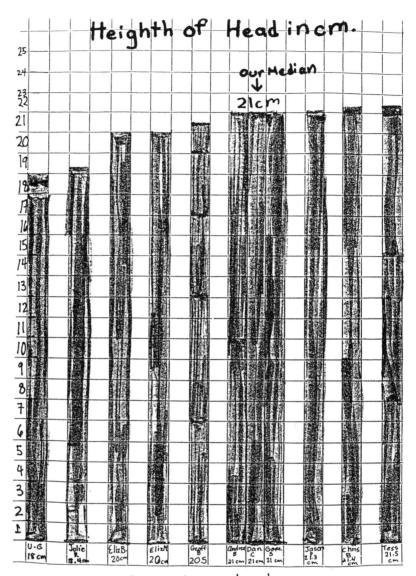

Figure 5–2.
Graph of head height
measurements.

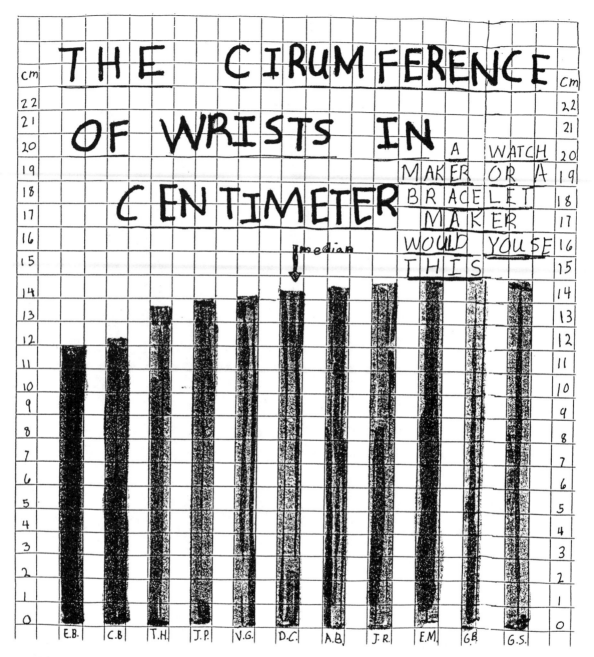

Figure 5–3.
Graph of wrist
circumference
measurements.

Describing Activities with Numbers

Most children are used to hearing sports statistics, so the idea of using numbers to describe things one can do will not be surprising to them. Before beginning these activities, ask them about their favorite sports, teams, and players and whether they know any sports facts that involve numbers.

IN SCHOOL: PERSONAL SPORTS AND INDIVIDUAL FEATS

The playground or gym is a good place to answer the following:

- *How many times* can you jump rope, bounce a ball, shoot consecutive baskets without missing?
- *How long does it take* to walk, run, skip, or jump a certain distance marked off in the gym or on the playground?
- *How high* can you reach or jump? (Tape some paper to the wall, then have the children dip the tips of their middle fingers in paint or rub them on an ink pad; as they reach or jump up, they can touch the paper with their fingers, leaving a mark.
- *How long* can you hum one note, stand on one foot (with eyes open and with eyes closed), hold up a heavy object with one arm, or stand on your head?
- *How much* can you expand your chest? (After the students exhale as much air as they can, let them take one another's chest measurements. Then ask them to inhale as much as they can and measure their chests again. The air in their lungs accounts for the difference.)
- *What is your heart rate?* Show your students how to take their pulse (the big artery on the side of the neck is the easiest place to find it). Ask them to count how many times their heart beats in fifteen or thirty seconds and in one minute. Then let them experiment with finding their pulse rates when resting, after jumping up and down fifty times, and after running across the playground and back. With the help of a calculator for multiplying, the children can find out how many times their heart beats in an hour, a day, a week, a month, a year, or even in their lifetimes!

AT HOME: COUNTING, MEASURING, TIMING

Parents may be able to help children gather facts about the following activities, which are more easily carried out at home:

- How many steps do you climb each day?
- How many blocks do you walk to school?
- How many miles do you ride to school, in the school bus or on your bike?
- *(In the city)* How many steps does it take you to walk around your block?
- *(In the country)* How many steps does it take you to walk to your mailbox?
- How long does it take you to do family chores?
- What is your top biking speed?

Some children may also want to record personal sports statistics.

BACK IN SCHOOL: A TYPICAL CLASS MEMBER

By this time your class's personal record books will be brimming with numbers. Each book is a unique portrait of one person. How typical is that person? From the information the students have gathered they can put together a portrait of an average class member.

Start out with a discussion: From all the things the children have recorded, let them choose ten characteristics, such as height, number of brothers and sisters, resting heart rate, and so on. Write these across the top of large sheets of paper so that each student can write down his or her numbers for the listed characteristics. Then divide the class into five groups and let each group choose two of the characteristics to work on.

For younger children, this may mean simply choosing a number somewhere between the largest and smallest on the list. Older children can determine the mean, median, and mode and decide which of these three would be most appropriate to use.

Start a personal number book for your typical class member. Groups can enter information about their typical classmate as they derive it. Your class might also want to create a portrait of this mythical class member, which can preside over your room or represent your class in the hallway outside.

Gauging Growth

Each child's height and weight were measured at birth and in most families continue to be measured periodically when children are taken for check-ups. Some parents will have kept these records. Height and weight may also have been measured and recorded in school. Many arithmetical computations can be done with such records, and these computations will allow children to trace their own development.

IN SCHOOL: KEEPING HEIGHT AND WEIGHT RECORDS

Height and weight can be measured when school begins in September and again periodically throughout the year. See whether you can arrange for the students to use a doctor's scale with an attached height-measuring device. The nurse's office probably has one that can be used either there or in your classroom. Make sure that the students have a chance to participate in making their own measurements. If you don't have access to a doctor's scale, an ordinary bathroom scale and a five-foot tape measure attached to the wall will do. Although many bathroom scales are marked in both pounds and kilograms, it's fun to have two separate scales. The students can weigh themselves on both scales, compare their weights in kilograms with their weights in pounds, and begin to get a feeling of weight as expressed in both kinds of units.

Set a regular schedule for recording measurements—on the first school day of each month, for example—so that students will be able to figure out their rates of growth (so many inches or centimeters per month). Give each student a folder containing a blank height and weight chart and two forms for height and weight graphs, which can be added to each month.

AT HOME: RECORDS FROM THE PAST

Ask parents to share with their children any records they have kept of their children's height and weight. If they don't have any, it is possible they could obtain them from their doctor or clinic. Some children may be able to write down a height and weight for each year of their lives and bring this information to school.

BACK IN SCHOOL: DESCRIBING GROWTH

If children lack personal statistics for some of the years they were enrolled in their current school, help them obtain the information from the school office. They can use the information from home and from the records they have been keeping in school to answer such questions as:

"How tall am I? How much do I weigh?"

- How much have you grown since birth, in height and weight?
- How many times as tall or heavy are you now?
- By what percentage has your height or weight increased since birth?
- What has your growth rate been during your life? (How many inches or centimeters did you grow on the average each year?)
- What has your growth rate been this year (in inches or centimeters per month)?

Children who have continuous records can also answer these questions:

- At what period of your life did you grow the fastest?
- How long did it take you to double your birth weight and length?

Calculators will be of great help in some of these computations, but they may be a hindrance in others (in subtracting one measurement in feet and inches from another feet-and-inches measurement, for example). Deciding whether or not to use them should be part of the thinking and problem solving your students will have to do.

More Investigations for Home and School

Some kinds of investigation can be carried out equally well at home or at school. The questions in this section offer many opportunities for older children to practice measurement and at the same time prompt family members to look at themselves in a new way. Not all children will want to explore all these homework questions, but given enough time and encouragement, your students should bring plenty of interesting information back to school.

HOW MUCH WEIGHT DO YOU GAIN DURING DINNER?

At home children can weigh themselves before and after they eat, or just after they get up in the morning and again after their evening meal. They can also weigh themselves with and without clothes, compare their weights wearing winter and summer clothes, and record all these measurements so they can discuss them with their classmates.

CLOTHING SIZES

Copy the body measurement chart shown in Figure 5–4 and send it home together with some questions and suggestions for activities:

- Do your sizes and measurements match those given on the chart?
- Check all your clothing, including shoes, and list the sizes you found. (If you wish, you can ask other family members for permission to check their clothing sizes, too.)
- Look at the sizes in a man's dress shirt, pants or jeans. What do the numbers mean?
- How and when did clothing sizes originate?

HOW TO GET THE CORRECT SIZE

Concerned about fit? Don't be. Our clothing is generously cut. Just order your usual size.

Hats: Measure around head with tape above brow ridges. Convert inches to hat size using chart below.

Neck: Take a shirt with a collar that fits you well. Lay collar flat, and measure from center of collar button to far end of button hole. Number of inches = size.

Arm: Bend elbow, and measure from center of neck (backside) to elbow and down to wrist. Number of inches = size.

Chest: Measure around fullest part of chest, keeping tape up under arms and around shoulder blades.

Waist: Measure around waist, at the height you normally wear your slacks. Keep one finger between tape and body. Number of inches = size.

Inseam: Take a pair of pants that fits you well. Measure from the crotch seam to bottom of pants. Number of inches (to the nearest ½") = inseam length. We inseam free!

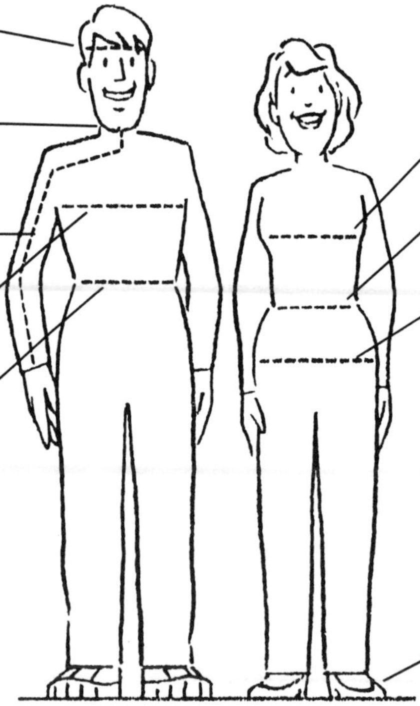

Bust: Measure around fullest part of bust, keeping tape up under arms and around shoulder blades.

Waist: Measure around waist. Keep one finger between tape and body.

Hips: Stand with heels together, and measure around fullest part.

Belts: Order the same size belt as your pant waist size. If between "even" sizes, order the next larger size.

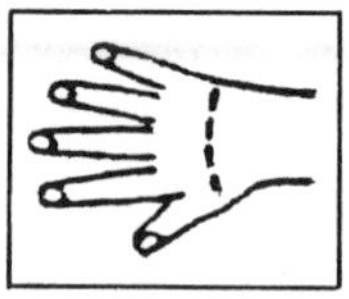

Gloves: Measure around hand at fullest part (exclude thumb). If right-handed, use right hand, and vice versa. Number of inches = size.

Shoes: Use your street shoe size.

Men's

HEIGHT:
Short	5'3"–5'7"
Regular	5'8"–6'0"
Tall	6'1"–6'3"

	Small		Medium		Large		X-Large		XX-Large	
Neck	14	14½	15	15½	16	16½	17	17½	18	18½
Chest	34	36	38	40	42	44	46	48	50	52
Waist	28	30	32	34	36	38	40	42	44	46
Arm (Reg.)	32½	33	33½	34	34½	35	35½	36	36½	37
Arm (Tall)	34	34½	35	35½	36	36½	37	37½	38	38½

Women's

HEIGHT:
Petite	4'11"–5'3"
Regular	5'4"–5'7"
Tall	5'8"–5'11"

	X-Small		Small		Medium		Large		X-Large		XX-Large	
	4	6	8	10	12	14	16	18	20	22	24
Bust	33	34	35	36	37½	39	40½	42½	44½	46½	48½
Waist	24½	25½	26½	27½	29	30½	32	34	36	38	40
Hip	35½	36½	37½	38½	40	41½	43	45	47	49	51
Arm (Pet.)	28	28¾		29½		30¼		31		31¾	
Arm (Reg.)	29	29¾		30½		31¼		32		32¾	
Arm (Tall)	30	30¾		31½		32¼		33		33¾	

Hats

Head Size:	21½"	21⅞"	22¼"	22⅝"	23"	23½"	23⅞"	24¼"
Hat Size:	6⅞	7	7⅛	7¼	7⅜	7½	7⅝	7¾
Order Size:	Small		Medium		Large		X-Large	

Unisex Sizing
We carry some items with unisex sizing. Please refer to the catalog copy to find your correct size in those products.

Men's Sportjacket Sizing

Chest Size	36	37	38	39	40	41	42	43/44
Coat Size	38	39	40	41	42	43	44	46
Short 5'3"-5'7"		*		*		*		
Reg. 5'8"-6'0"	*	*	*	*	*	*	*	*
Long 6'1"-6'3"			*	*	*	*	*	*

* means we stock sportjackets in these sizes.

Children's

HEIGHT:
Child should stand in stocking feet, with feet together, back to a wall. Measurement from crown of head to the floor = height.

CHEST WAIST HIPS:
Use the directions for Adults shown above.

Infants

Size	3 month	6 month	12 month	18 month	24 month
Weight	up to 13 lbs.	14-18 lbs.	19-22 lbs.	22½-25½ lbs.	26-29 lbs.
Height	up to 24"	25"-27"	27½"-29"	29½"-31"	31½"-33"

Toddler Girl
	2T	3T	4T
Height	33	36	39
Chest	21	22	23
Waist	20	20½	21
Hip	21	22	23

Little Girl
	4	5	6	6X
Height	39	42	45	47
Chest	23	23½	24½	25½
Waist	21	21½	22	22½
Hip	23	24	25	26

Girl
	7	8	10	12	14
Height	49	52	55	58	60
Chest	26	27	28	30	32
Waist	22½	23	24	25	26
Hip	27	28	30	32	34

Toddler Boy
	2T	3T	4T
Height	33	36	39
Chest	21	22	23
Waist	20	20½	21
Hip	21	22	23

Little Boy
	4	5	6	7
Height	39	42	45	49
Chest	23	23½	24½	25½
Waist	21	21½	22	22½
Hip	23	24	25	26

Boy
	8	10	12	14	16
Height	52	55	59	62	64
Chest	27	28	30	32	33
Waist	23	24	25	26	27½
Hip	27	28	29	31	33

Figure 5–4.
(*opposite*) Body measurement chart from a *Lands' End* catalog.

Reading the Numbers by Mary Blocksma (1989) has some useful information on this topic on pages 33–37. An amusing account of the origin of shoe sizes can be found on pages 61–62.

RELATIONSHIPS BETWEEN BODY MEASUREMENTS

- In your family, are foot lengths the same as shoe sizes? Are shoe and sock sizes the same? If they are not the same, can you see any connection?
- Do people in your family with small feet also have small hands?
- Try this old trick: Take the foot part of a sock and see if it fits around your fist. If it does, the sock is supposed to be the right size. Does this work for you and your family?
- With a soft tape measure or a piece of string, take the following measurements: around the base of your thumb, around your wrist, around your neck, and around your waist. Is there a relationship between the numbers or between the lengths of the pieces of string?
- There is another old saying: "Once around the waist, twice around the neck. Once around the neck, twice around the wrist." Is this true for you?
- Are you or family members "square" persons? Measure your height and the width of your arm span. Use these to make a scale drawing of yourself with arms outstretched. Then draw a rectangle just touching the top of your head, your fingertips and your feet (see Figure 5–5). Do you fit into a square? If not, how would you describe yourself?
- Which part of your arm is longer, from your elbow to your shoulder or from your elbow to your wrist? What if you include your hand?
- What is the ratio of your forearm to your upper arm? Do other people in the class or family have the same ratio?

Figure 5–5.
A "square" person and a "rectangular" person.

Figure 5–6.
"Am I ready for school?"

■ In a number of African countries, children are considered ready for school if they can reach over the top of their head with an arm and touch the opposite ear. (The head-arm ratio changes as they grow.) Is everyone in your class "ready for school?"

FOUR WAYS TO MEASURE YOUR HAND

Sometimes there are several different ways to measure one thing. How many ways are there to measure your hand?

1. You can measure the *length,* from wrist to tip of longest finger, and also the *width.*

2. You can also measure the *area* of your hand: Place one hand on a sheet of graph paper, palm down and fingers open, and trace

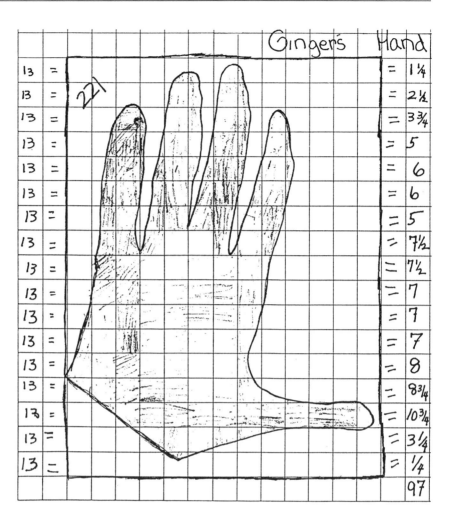

Figure 5–7.
The area of Ginger's hand.

around it with a pencil. Then count the squares. (You will have to decide how to count partial squares.) If you are using centimeter graph paper, the count of the squares will give you the area of your hand in square centimeters (cm^2). If you are using quarter-inch graph paper, outline a one-inch square and you will see that it contains sixteen quarter-inch squares. Divide the number of squares covered by sixteen to get the area covered by your hand in square inches. (Fifth graders Ginger, Mollie, and Mo each took a different approach to solving this problem—see Figures 5–7, 5–8, and 5–9.)

3. You can also measure your hand's *volume* (the amount of space it takes up) by seeing how much water your fist displaces. Put some water in a glass jar and mark the water line with tape or marker. Submerge your fist into the water up to your wrist and record the new water line. The amount of water between the two lines is a measure of the volume of your fist. You could pour this

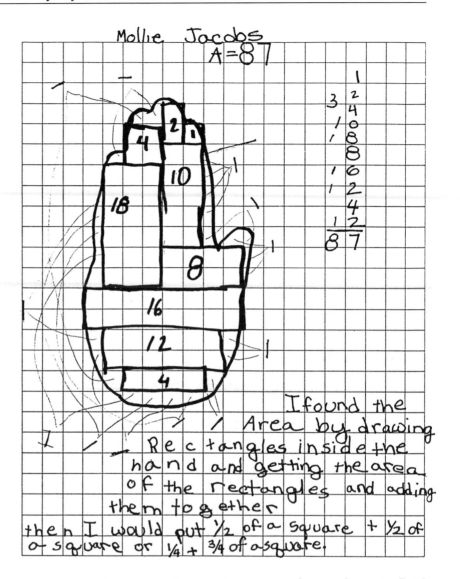

Figure 5–8.
The area of Mollie's hand.

amount into a measuring cup to see your fist's volume in fluid ounces or milliliters.

4. Finally you could measure *how much your hand can hold*. Fill a bowl with small beans—like soy beans or black turtle beans—and see how many you can hold in each hand. Do the right and left hand hold the same number of beans?

How do these four hand measurements compare?

There is no end to personal statistics. The previous long list of suggested activities may grow even longer once you and the children start adding your own ideas. Mathematics becomes much more interesting to children when they begin to see the role it plays in their lives.

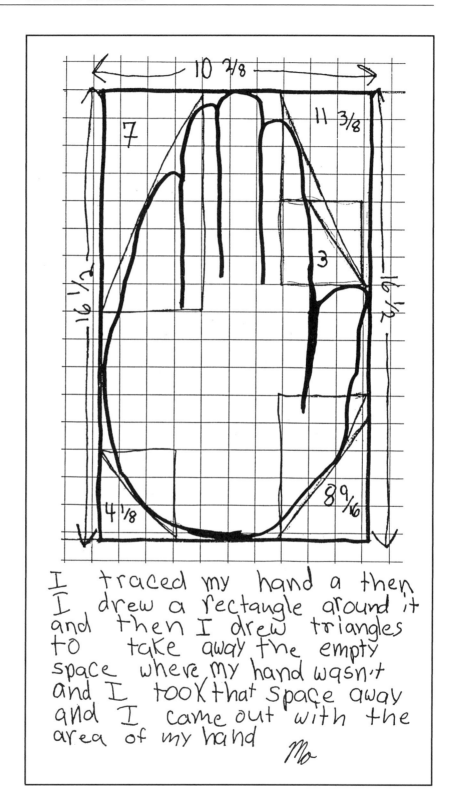

I traced my hand a then
I drew a rectangle around it
and then I drew triangles
to take away the empty
space where my hand wasn't
and I took that space away
and I came out with the
area of my hand   Mo

Figure 5–9.
The area of Mo's
hand.

Chapter 6   Supermarket Shopping

6
Supermarket Shopping

Some people like to go shopping, others hate it. It depends, of course, on what you are going to buy. Clothes for yourself or for your kids? A labor-saving appliance or some seedlings for your garden? Or the weekly groceries—once again. The popularity of pizza parlors, fast-food restaurants, frozen dinners, and deli departments in supermarkets, as well as the growing availability of take-out foods at restaurants, are a good indication that many people try to avoid regular grocery-shopping trips. Taking young kids along on shopping expeditions can make this weekly chore even more trying.

If, however, you are looking for readily available opportunities to practice mathematical thinking, the supermarket is a wonderful place. Almost the entire elementary school math curriculum could be taught around supermarket topics! You can help parents view grocery shopping in a new way by suggesting interesting and challenging supermarket math activities for their children.

Matching in the Supermarket

In Chapter 7, children are encouraged to do one-to-one matching: pots and lids, cups and saucers, straws and milk cartons, and so on. The matching we are suggesting in the supermarket is simpler.

IN SCHOOL: MATCHING LABELS OF CANS AND BOXES

Collect a variety of empty boxes of cereal, crackers, Jell-O, and so on, as well as empty cans with removable wrappers or with pictures on them. You need to have two of each product, a wrapper and an empty can for instance, or two empty boxes or cans. A short note to parents (see Figure 6–1) will help you build up your collection and also inform parents of this project. Additional information on matching can be found in "Matching in the Kitchen" (Chapter 7) and in

Figure 6–1.
Letter to parents
about learning math
in the supermarket.
(A reproducible
master for this form
letter in included in
the Appendix.)

Dear Parents,

We are trying to see in how many different ways we can use the supermarket to study math. We want to start with matching, an important early math activity. Even before children can read, they can recognize products by their labels. I would like the children to learn how to find things in the supermarket by taking labels removed from cans or cut from boxes and matching them with the identical labels on products displayed on the shelves. I hope that your youngsters will soon be able to help you with your grocery shopping!

Please send us some empty cans and food boxes (two of each individual product) to make a display in the classroom so that the children can practice matching. Thank you for your help.

Sincerely,

"Matching, Sorting, and Classifying" (Chapter 2). You could attach relevant excerpts from those sections to the above letter.

When you have an adequate number and variety of food containers, you or a few children can make a display with one of the two available sets. Take wrappers off cans and cut the fronts out of boxes in the other set. Give these labels to one or two children at a time. They can now go "shopping" by finding the products that match their labels.

AT HOME: MATCHING LABELS IN THE SUPERMARKET

After children have had some time to practice this kind of matching in school, you can let parents know that their kids are ready to help them with grocery shopping. Armed with parts of empty boxes and a couple of labels from cans, the children can look for the identical items on the supermarket shelves. (See Figure 6–2.) It might be a good idea to send home another note reminding parents to help their children find the proper aisles when they start "shopping." After several shopping trips, the children will begin to know the general layout of the store.

BACK IN SCHOOL: WHERE DID YOU FIND THIS CEREAL BOX?

After the children have been on a number of shopping trips with their families, have them tell you about their experiences. Did they enjoy searching for products? Ask them *how* they found things. When the children are talking about this, try to raise some questions that will help them think about *why* things are arranged in a certain way:

Andre Cotto

Figure 6–2.
A supermarket
search.

- Which items were in the same aisles, which were in different aisles?
- Which things were generally found close to each other?
- How many different aisles did you have to go to to find the things you were asked to get?
- Were there products you couldn't reach?
- What products were on the top and the bottom shelves? Can you think of a reason why they were placed there?
- Where were frozen and refrigerated products stored?
- Why do you think magazines and candy are displayed near the checkout counters?
- What are the main categories of the goods sold in your supermarket?

Questions like these will make children aware that there are reasons behind the organization of supermarkets.

How Are Supermarkets Organized?

SCHOOL PROJECT:
BUILDING A STORE IN THE CLASSROOM

When children go shopping with their families, they get to know the "public" areas of the store. A trip to the supermarket to see where food is delivered, where meat is stored and prepared for the display cases, where produce is trimmed and packaged, would add greatly to the children's understanding. If a trip is not possible, parents might ask the manager if he or she could let their child see some of these areas.

Questions raised in the previous section were intended to get children to think about the reasons different food items are placed where they are. To get the answers to some of the questions, older children can try to talk to the store manager. It will be interesting to have students compare the information they receive from managers or other store employees.

In order to create a grocery store in their classroom, children will have to think and make decisions about how to organize it. This is a challenging class activity that gives children a chance to process newly acquired information. Conducting discussions, writing, organizing information in charts and graphs, expressing feelings and ideas in artwork, are all ways in which children relive and rethink new experiences. Building a supermarket in their classroom, either with wooden blocks or with a variety of cartons, will require students of all ages to think critically about their task. (If you don't have sufficient space in your room to have the children build on the floor, a smaller table model or even a mural will make a good substitute.)

To start out, let the children form groups and ask them to come up with a floor plan. Each group will present their plan to the class, giving reasons for the layout they chose. The class then must decide which plan (or combination of plans) will work best. A great deal of logical thinking will be necessary before the children will be able to present and justify their layout decisions.

Since such a building project will take time, it is important to clear an area of the room where blocks or cartons can be left out. When the basic structures of the supermarket have been built, children can use their imagination to create the needed people and props. They will get an intuitive sense of proportion and scale as they make shoppers, food products, and other items for their store.

Counting in the Supermarket

HOME PROJECT: COUNTING PEOPLE, FOOD ITEMS, AND OTHER THINGS

Children's enthusiasm for counting can be freely exercised in the supermarket. They can be happily engaged in counting things for at least part of the family shopping trip. What is there to count? Here are some suggestions to share with parents:

People

- How many people are there in this aisle?
- How many children are there in this aisle and in the two adjoining aisles?
- How many little children are riding in shopping carts?
- How many people are waiting in our checkout line?
- How many people are in the longest line? the shortest?
- How many cashiers and baggers are working at this time?

Food items

- How many different brands of yogurt can you count?
- How many different varieties of apples are displayed?
- How many sizes of your favorite cereal can you find?

Other things

- How many checkout lanes are there?
- How many are open at this time?
- How many different magazines are on the racks by the checkout counter?

Figure 6–3. "What I counted in the supermarket" chart. (A reproducible master for this form is included in the Appendix.)

WHAT I COUNTED IN THE SUPERMARKET

Name of the Store _King Coopers_

Day of the Week _Saturday_   Time of Day _10:01 am_

WHAT I COUNTED	HOW MANY
Kids in carts	12
Jars of Apple Sauce	24
Garbage on floor	4

Send home a copy of the chart shown in Figure 6–3 and ask parents of younger children to record the results for them. Older children can keep their own tally while they are counting.

Here are a few of our favorite counting books for children. You will find many more in most libraries.

Anno's Counting Book, by Mitsumasa Anno, 1977 (New York: Crowell).

Over in the Meadow, by John Langstaff and Feodor Rojankovsky, 1961 (New York: Harcourt Brace).

Ten, Nine, Eight, by Molly Bang, 1989 (Orlando, FL: Harcourt Brace Jovanovich).

Trucks You Can Count On, by Doug Magee, 1986 (New York: Dodd, Mead).

Shapes in the Supermarket

A great variety of shapes can be found in the supermarket. A supermarket shape hunt might be a good activity for your students after they have studied shapes in school and in home kitchens. (See "Shapes Everywhere" in Chapter 7.)

IN SCHOOL: SHAPE REVIEW

See how many two-dimensional or three-dimensional shapes your students can name. (Discussions of shapes by third graders are included as Figures 6–4 and 6–5.) Make a list of the shapes they remember seeing in the supermarket.

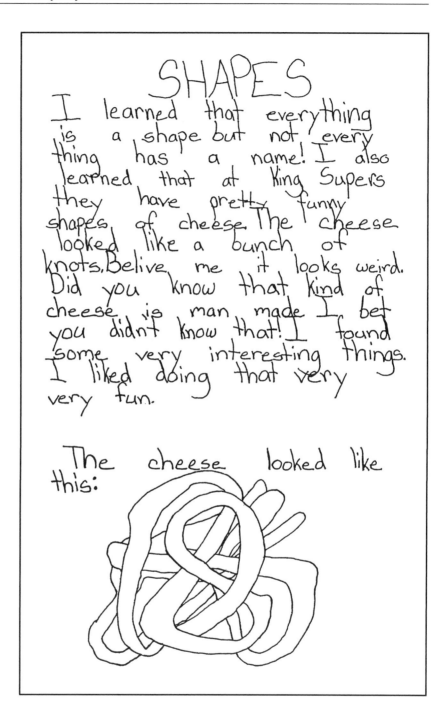

SHAPES

I learned that everything is a shape but not every thing has a name! I also learned that at King Supers they have pretty funny shapes of cheese. The cheese looked like a bunch of knots. Belive me it looks weird. Did you know that kind of cheese is man made I bet you didn't know that! I found some very interesting things. I liked doing that very very fun.

The cheese looked like this:

Figure 6–4.
Jamie's "shapes" story.

I found lots of shapes that had no name. I did't no there so many shapes in the store. My favorite shape was the banana with I called cresent moon. I also liked the shape cube we found many cubes. I think we found a very interesting thing which was a marshmellow which I called a pillow.

Figure 6–5. Christy's "shapes" story.

Third graders looking for shapes on a trip to the supermarket.

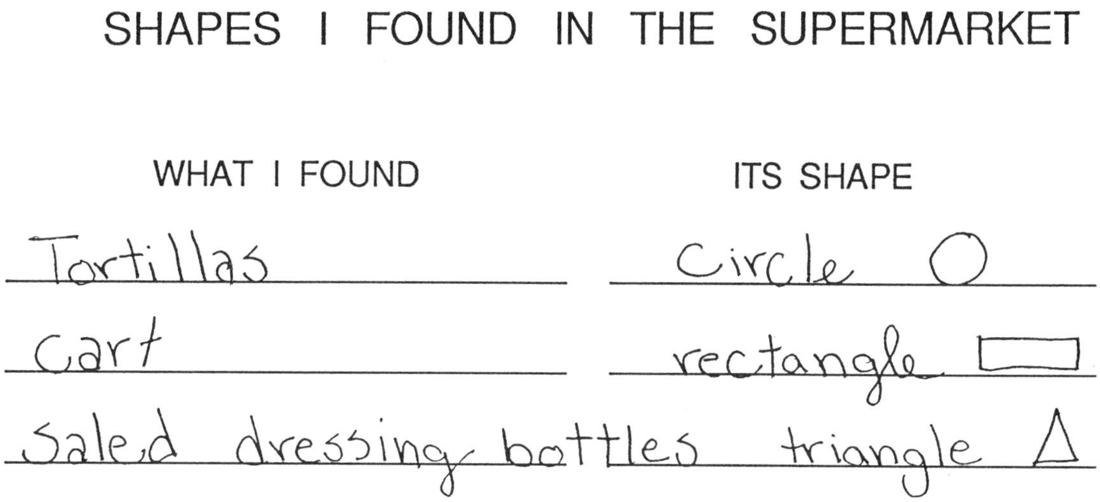

SHAPES I FOUND IN THE SUPERMARKET

WHAT I FOUND　　　　　　　　　　ITS SHAPE

Tortillas　　　　　　　　　Circle ○

Cart　　　　　　　　　　　rectangle ▭

Saled dressing bottles　triangle △

Figure 6–6.
"Shapes I found in the supermarket" form. (A reproducible master for this form is included in the Appendix.)

AT HOME: LOOKING FOR MORE SHAPES

Ask your students to look for additional shapes on their next shopping trip, and have them record their findings. Suggest, for example, that they look for different shapes of crackers—there are square, round, rectangular, elliptical, triangular, and hexagonal crackers on the shelves—as well as shapes in the produce department and shapes of various types of packaging. Give the students a copy of the sheet shown in Figure 6–6 on which to record their findings.

BACK IN SCHOOL:
MAN-MADE AND NATURAL SHAPES

When the lists come back to school, ask the students to put all the information from their recording sheets onto a single chart with two categories: "Shapes Found in Nature" and "Shapes Made by People and Machines." (Two such charts made by individual children are shown in Figures 6–7 and 6–8.)

Figure 6–7.
Matt's shape
drawings.

Figure 6–8.
Mikki's shape drawings.

Here are some additional questions for discussion:

- Which man-made shapes did you see most frequently?
- Which shapes of fruits and vegetables were most common?
- How many different shapes of fruits and vegetables did you find?
- Were there shapes of produce for which you had no name?
- What shape name would you give to a banana or a butternut squash?
- Can you think of names for other unnamed shapes?

Getting students to think about the different shapes may well lead to additional questions such as, Why are most cans cylindrical? Why are so many fruits round? Why are boxes rectangular?

ADDITIONAL ACTIVITY: ARRANGING SHAPES

After talking about shapes in general, a new shape focus can be introduced:

- How are the different shapes of canned, packaged, and frozen foods stored on the shelves?
- Are some shapes easier to store than others?
- How are fruits and vegetables displayed?

Ask children to think about this topic the next time they go to the supermarket. If possible, ask each student to bring to school one orange, one small can of tomato paste, and one box of Jell-O. (Be sure you tell parents that the tomato paste and the Jell-O will be sent back home!) Let the children experiment with displaying these items in various ways. What can they learn from making these arrangements?

How Much Does This Bag of Potatoes Weigh?

Lots of things in the supermarket have to be weighed at the checkout counter, and most packages and cans have the net weight printed on the label. For young children it is not important to know *how much* something weighs in pounds or ounces; these measurement units don't have much meaning until children have developed a sense of what is "heavy" and what is "light." The supermarket offers numerous opportunities for sensory experiences with weight. Standardized weight units, introduced later in school, will make more sense to children who have been encouraged to feel the different weights of products purchased by their families.

Although she didn't find this brick in a supermarket, a first-grade girl's face and body give a clear indication of its weight!

IN SCHOOL: WHICH IS HEAVIER? WHICH WEIGHS MORE? HOW MUCH DOES IT WEIGH?

A simple but sturdy pan balance can be used to let young children experiment with weight. Put out a collection of things from the supermarket—an orange, a box of cereal, a small head of cabbage, a can of tuna, a package of spaghetti, a cupful of peanuts, and so on. The youngest children can address the question, Which of two objects is heavier, which is lighter? Let the children first feel the weight of the different items in their hands and then use the pan balance to see which is heavier. After some experimentation, ask them to predict which of two objects will be heavier or lighter.

If children have developed a sense of weight and have begun to understand that words like "heavy" and "light" are relative, ask them to use the balance to arrange three items in order of increasing weight. The children are still comparing weights, but now they have to think more deeply about it.

A first-grade boy and his teacher use a balance to determine relative weights.

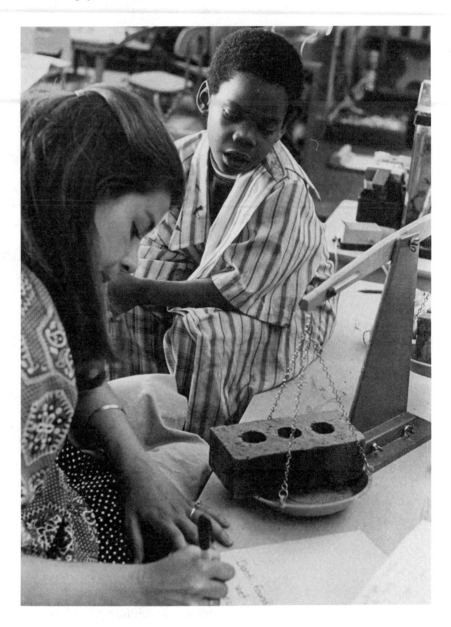

If your students are already using nonstandard measuring units, they can actually weigh your collection of supermarket objects. If they are unfamiliar with nonstandard units of weight, you can now introduce this topic. There are many possible nonstandard units children can use. Washers of different sizes work very well but you can also use marbles, nails, or any other objects that come in one or more sizes. When children weigh objects with units, they have begun to deal with the question, How much does it weigh? This apple, for instance, weighs twenty-one washers or nine marbles.

For older children who have used standard measuring units, it would be nice to have a regular kitchen scale or a hanging spring balance similar to those found in supermarkets. These students can then check the weight marked on packaged produce, on cans, and on cardboard boxes.

AT HOME: THINKING OF WEIGHT WHILE SHOPPING IN THE SUPERMARKET

Depending on the age of the children you teach, you can suggest some of the following activities to parents. You could also send home photocopies of the sections on measurement from Chapter 2 to help parents understand how children gradually learn what weighing is all about.

The activities suggested below are arranged in order of increasing difficulty.

- Ask your children to feel the weight of a bag of potatoes and of a package of potato chips before they place them in the shopping cart. Then have them pick out two other items of very different weights.
- Ask your child to push the shopping cart and comment on its weight as you are filling it up. Is it harder to push now? How would it feel if it were filled with toilet paper or cereal boxes? What if we bought only potatoes or oranges today? Encourage parents to make similar comments to give children practice with noticing and experiencing different weights.
- Ask your child to find two packages marked with the same weight—for instance, five pounds of flour and five pounds of onions, or one pound of sugar and one pound of mushrooms. Then you can ask, Do they feel the same? Are the packages the same size?
- In the produce department, there are scales on which you can weigh the produce you are buying. Children who have experience with standard units of weight can help you fill the bags and estimate when they have reached the desired weight. You can ask them, for instance, to get one pound of tomatoes, five pounds of

apples, a two-pound head of cabbage, and so on. This will provide good practice in dealing with weights.

■ Ask children to estimate the weight of a cantaloupe, a large squash or eggplant, or, if they are strong enough, a watermelon. Their estimate may be way off at first, but with practice and experience, their guesses will come closer to the actual weight.

Additional weight questions will come to mind as you, the parents, and the children focus on this topic.

Where Do Bananas Come From? Distance, Time, and Price

Few of us pay much attention to where the foods we purchase come from. We look at quality and price and make our selection. Only under special circumstances do we become aware of where the produce we are buying originated. If a frost in Florida kills a large percentage of the orange crop, we know that the prices will suddenly shoot up; a dock strike may affect the price of bananas as they lie rotting on the pier; a pesticide scare in one part of the country will lower prices dramatically as people all over stop buying that particular crop. If we looked at the crates in which much of the produce is shipped, we would be surprised to find out how far some fruits and vegetables have traveled.

Not only produce comes from far away; many of our supermarkets have food from all over the world: Italian olive oil, Colombian coffee, Chinese noodles, Norwegian crackers, French cheese, or Mexican chili peppers, just to mention a few. Canned and packaged food and produce also comes from various parts of the United States.

A supermarket geography project will help children gain a better understanding of the distance some of their food has traveled before it ended up on the stores' shelves.

IN SCHOOL: SUPERMARKET GEOGRAPHY

Ask your students if they have ever noticed foreign labels on produce crates and on bottles, cans, and packaged food. Have them talk about where they think the food comes from and how it gets to their supermarkets. Tell them that you want to study where, in this country and in other parts of the world, food is grown, processed, and packaged, and how long it takes to get from its place of origin to your community.

AT HOME: WHERE DOES MY FOOD COME FROM?

Ask children to look through their kitchen cabinets and write down where some of the things came from. On their next trip to the supermarket, have them look at produce in crates to find out where it came from. If children have time and parents' permission to wander around the store, see if they can find some things that came from another country. Ask them to keep lists of their findings.

BACK IN SCHOOL:
HOW FAR HAS MY FOOD TRAVELED?

Large maps of the United States and of the world can be mounted on a bulletin board, if possible near a table. Children can draw pictures of the food, cut out pictures from magazines, or use wrappers and empty boxes and cans to show what they found. A piece of string can be taped to any of the above and attached with a map pin to the appropriate place on the U.S. or world map. When the display is complete, children can figure out what distance the food has traveled. These are questions older children can research:

- How long did it take the different foods to come here?
- What mode of transportation was used? (Trucks? Trains? Ships? Air freight?)
- Did the product have to be refrigerated in transit?
- Do grapes that come from another country cost more than grapes grown in the United States? If so, why? If not, why not?
- Is produce that travels a long distance more expensive than produce grown locally?

Some of these questions will have to be answered by supermarket employees. If children are sufficiently interested in this subject, you might arrange a final trip to the supermarket. In preparation for such a trip, children can form different groups and brainstorm questions covering all the supermarket topics that have been studied. On the trip, if you can set it up this way, the groups could interview different employees to get answers to their questions. Visit the supermarket before you take the children there, tell the manager about your project, and give him or her copies of the children's questions ahead of time.

Computing Unit Prices: Division

Comparing unit prices is generally the most efficient way to determine which of several products is the most economical. To aid the shopper, most large supermarkets now display unit prices on their shelves along with the total price of each item. The consumer, however, must be able to read and understand what unit prices signify. Knowing how unit prices are computed will enable children to use them effectively.

IN SCHOOL: HOW MUCH DOES ONE APPLE COST?

Supermarkets often offer both loose and packaged fruits at different prices. If you can, buy two quantities of the same brand of apples at different prices. Show them to your class. "Yesterday I bought these prebagged apples for $2.89 and this bag of loose apples for $2.75. Which bag do you think was a better buy?"

Initially the less expensive bag may seem more economical. If no one suggests figuring out the price of an individual apple, you can propose this yourself. Together, count the apples and give small groups the problem of determining the price of a single apple from each bag. Dividing the total cost by the number of apples is probably the most direct procedure. (Don't be surprised, however, if some groups come up with equally effective but less efficient methods, such as estimating the price of an apple, multiplying by the number of apples, and adjusting the estimate if the product is too large or too small.) Compare results as well as the strategies used. Then you can discuss which method produced an answer in the shortest time. If the children are using calculators for division, remind them to round off the results to the nearest cent.

If, in your initial discussion, the students didn't think of comparing the cost of one pound of apples, ask them how prices could have been compared if they had not been able to open the bags to count the individual apples.

AT HOME: A SHOPPING DECISION

Duplicate a supermarket advertisement showing a product offered in two different quantities at different prices. Ask the children to take this home and ask family members which one they would buy, and why. They should write down the responses.

BACK IN SCHOOL: COMPUTING UNIT PRICES

The students can now share their families' responses to the advertisement. What was the basis on which most people made their decisions?

Did they estimate or compute the cost of one item, pound, or ounce? What other considerations influenced their choices: amount needed? storage space? perishability?

Tell the students you are going to compare some other products just on the basis of cost. At different locations in the room place pairs of food containers in two sizes, with price labels attached. Hand out sheets on which to record the weight or volume of each package and its price. Then ask the students to circulate so that they can inspect the containers and record their weights and volumes. When information has been gathered, students should compute the price of one unit of weight or volume for each package to the nearest cent, dividing the price by the weight or volume.

As a class, decide which size of each product is a better buy. If some prove to be equal you can talk about determining the price to the nearest tenth of a cent. Ask where the students have seen prices expressed in tenths of a cent (on gas pumps? supermarket shelves?). Suggest looking at the labels on the shelves the next time they go shopping in the supermarket to see whether the store displays unit prices and how they are written.

Some of these activities may raise questions families don't ordinarily consider. The children's investigations may not change family shopping habits, but they will have had many opportunities to experience mathematics in use. They will also have gained a good understanding of how a supermarket operates.

7
In the Kitchen

If you had to choose just one place in the home in which to support children's mathematical learning, you would probably pick the kitchen. Try to focus on math for a day as you spend time in your kitchen and you will soon realize that mathematics is part of almost every activity.

You *estimate* when you decide how much spaghetti to boil for dinner or whether you have enough sugar left to bake some cookies; you *measure* quantities of ingredients, oven or freezer temperatures, cooking time in the microwave; you *count* the number of plates, napkins, and glasses you put on the dinner table; you *compute* the roasting time of a twenty-pound turkey; you *read numbers* on dials, timers, recipes and clocks; you work with *fractions* when you divide a pie or halve a recipe; you deal with three-dimensional *geometric shapes* like cones (funnels), rectangular prisms (boxes), or cylinders (cans of food); you estimate *volume* when you choose a container for leftovers and you *create patterns* when you decorate a cake or arrange foods for special occasions. All these activities, and many more, make the kitchen an ideal place in which to introduce children to the mathematics of the everyday world.

Most children enjoy cooking or preparing uncooked foods both at home and in school. A "kitchen" in the classroom can be as central a place for learning as a kitchen in the home is a place for family activities. Some teachers set up small cooking areas in their classrooms where older children can prepare a variety of simple dishes on their own and younger children can work with the help of teachers or volunteers. If space or expense is a problem, teachers can share their cooking equipment, especially larger pots and pans, hot plates, or toaster ovens. These items can be stored on a cart that travels from class to class. If there is wall space for a good-sized pegboard, kitchen utensils such as measuring cups and spoons, funnels, strainers, hand beaters, apple corers, and egg slicers can all be stored there, clearly visible and readily accessible.

By becoming involved in food-preparation projects, parents and their children can see that mathematics exists outside as well as in school and is very much part of everyone's daily life.

Matching in the Kitchen

Matching is an important early math activity. When children match one object with another object, they put them into one-to-one correspondence. One object from one bunch of stuff is matched with one object from another bunch of stuff. This skill has to be fully developed before children can learn to count with understanding. Parents may not be aware that matching plays such an important role in their children's mathematical development, nor may they be familiar with the phrase "one-to-one correspondence." You can copy or summarize the paragraph on matching in Chapter 2 and include this information when you ask parents to encourage matching activities at home.

There are many opportunities, both at school and at home, for young children to practice one-to-one correspondence—a special kind of matching. *In school,* children learn that there is one hook for each coat, one container of paint for each paint brush, one basket of crayons for each table or one straw for each carton of milk. Lining up in pairs is a kind of matching, as is dividing up into groups: one child for the red group, one child for the blue group, and one child for the green group. *At home and in school,* children match things naturally in their play: they cover each doll with a blanket, put a little person in each toy car, match pairs of cards, or fit a puzzle piece into its proper place. The kitchen offers a particularly rich environment for one-to-one matching.

AT HOME: ONE-TO-ONE MATCHING

Encourage parents to let their youngsters match pots with lids, cups with saucers, knives with forks, or any other sets of objects they or the children can think of. By helping to set the table, young children will learn to put one place mat by each chair, one napkin and one plate on each place mat, one glass, one knife, one fork, and one spoon by each plate, and so on. At dinner time parents can emphasize that there is one roll, one baked potato, or one piece of pie for each member of the family. When the kids have exhausted matching possibilities in the kitchen and dining area, ask them to look in the rest of the house for further examples.

BACK IN SCHOOL: CREATING WORKSHEETS

As a follow-up, see whether the children want to create their own worksheets on which they can connect objects that belong together by drawing a line between them. On commercial worksheets, children are often asked to match objects that have a logical connection (for instance, rubber boots and umbrella, chicken and eggs, hammer and nails). Creating such a worksheet themselves requires more active thinking and develops greater understanding than just drawing lines between objects selected by someone else. At home, children will have practiced

Figure 7–1.
A first grader's
worksheet on
matching.

this kind of logical thinking with real objects as they have looked for things that go together. In school they will tell you about their discoveries and explain the connection between the matching objects.

Prepare a set of blank worksheets for the children and explain or review how the pairs of objects should be placed. Then ask the children to draw the objects or cut out magazine pictures to glue on the worksheets. (A worksheet created by a first grader is shown in Figure 7–1.) Their worksheets can then be photocopied so everyone can try them out. If the kids enjoy this activity, they can continue their search for logically matched objects throughout school and home and create additional worksheets.

Counting in the Kitchen

COUNTING IN RHYTHM

Young children love to show off their counting skills to almost any adult who will listen. The ability to count by rote does not necessarily indicate that children have grasped the full meaning of number. It does mean, however, that they have memorized the words we have given to numbers and that they enjoy reciting them in the correct order.

Children who know the number words and children who are still learning them enjoy counting along with actions like clapping, bouncing balls, or jumping rope. This kind of activity will be especially helpful to children who still mix up the order of the number words. It is also a good intermediate step between reciting the number words in order and learning to say the number words in sequence while pointing to or pushing aside one object at a time.

In school or home kitchens, children can count along when they stir, sift, or mix ingredients. Counting along is also useful when kids have to take turns. If the teacher says: "Everyone can stir twenty times" all the kids in the cooking group can count to twenty, at which time the stirrer passes on the mixing bowl without any problem. At home, this kind of counting can cut down on arguments among siblings.

Children seem to prefer manual implements to the faster and more efficient electric equipment. If you like to go to garage sales, you might find some castoffs the children would enjoy using. Parents may also have some to lend or contribute. An old-fashioned meat grinder is great for making peanut butter; a wooden coffee mill grinds wheat or rye kernels into flour; a hand orange juicer allows students to measure how much juice is produced by one squeeze or one orange; hand eggbeaters whip cream into delicious butter. There will be lots of counting and taking turns with activities like these.

COUNTING OBJECTS

As children develop a deeper understanding of numbers, they are able to count objects. At this stage, they enjoy counting all kinds of things. At school, they can count blocks, beads, buttons, pencils, crayons,

Dear Parents,

We've been practicing counting objects at school. You can help your child get more practice if you encourage him or her to count things in the course of your daily activities. In the kitchen, for instance, children can count the number of

- spoons in the drawer
- items you unpack from grocery bags
- ingredients used in a recipe
- utensils on the dinner table
- plates or glasses taken from the dishwasher

and so on.

Don't worry if your child makes mistakes like skipping a number or counting one object twice and another not at all. Try not to correct these at this stage of counting—such mistakes are quite common. Learning to count is a lengthy and complicated process, and only practice, time, and experience will teach your child to do it correctly.

See how many things you can find to count—in the kitchen and in the rest of your home!

Sincerely,

Figure 7–2.
Letter to parents about practicing counting in the kitchen. (A reproducible master for this form letter is included in the Appendix.)

books, and so on. When you are practicing counting at school, suggest to parents (see Figure 7–2) what things the children can count at home in the course of daily activities.

The stages that children go through before they can count with full understanding are described in Chapter 2 in the section on counting. This would be a good time to share this section with your parents, either orally or as an attachment to your letter.

A Kitchen Number Search

When young children begin to take an interest in reading numbers, they spot them everywhere. Teachers and parents can support this interest, guiding children to places where numbers are and helping them understand their functions.

IN SCHOOL: LOOKING FOR NUMBERS

Do a number search in your classroom and then continue your search in the building. Ask whether the custodian, a member of the kitchen staff, the nurse, and the school secretary could each spend a little time with small groups of children showing them numbers in their respective workplaces. A walk down the street would enlarge your list considerably.

On your search, the children may find at least three groups of numbers: numbers used for identification, numbers that count things, and numbers that designate measurements. Here are some examples:

Numbers used for identification

- In the classroom: numbers on library books and computer hardware.
- In the school building: numbers on classroom doors, on lockers, on gym equipment, on telephones.
- On the street: numbers on houses and streets, on license plates, on fire hydrants, on manhole covers, on postal boxes.

Numbers that count things

- In the classroom: numbers on the calendar (days since the first of the month), page numbers in books.
- In the school building: numbers on attendance and lunch records.
- On the street: numbers that tell you the population of a town, numbers on store signs (e.g., "3 for $1.00").

Numbers that measure something

- In the classroom: numbers on balances (weight), on thermometers (temperature), on rulers (length), on compasses (angles), on pencils (hardness), and on the classroom clock (time).
- In the school building: numbers on utility meters (rate of consumption), on kitchen stoves and freezers (temperature), on different types of scales (weight).
- On the street: numbers on road signs designating speed limits and distances to other towns, numbers on parking meters, numbers that tell you the altitude of a town or mountain pass.

Don't tell children these distinctions ahead of time. Start with a number search in your classroom and discuss the numbers found there. (One student found the numbers shown in Figure 7–3 in his kindergarten classroom.) See whether younger kids are aware of and help them to articulate the differences. Ask older students to list the numbers they find (in the classroom and in school and/or on a neighborhood walk) and to write down where they saw them. Divide the class into groups and ask them to create categories that would make it easier to study all these numbers. Have each group report how they classified the numbers, ask the class to discuss the outcomes, and help them chart the results. Did any of the groups make the main distinctions described above? If not, you can lead them to these basic classifications in a group discussion.

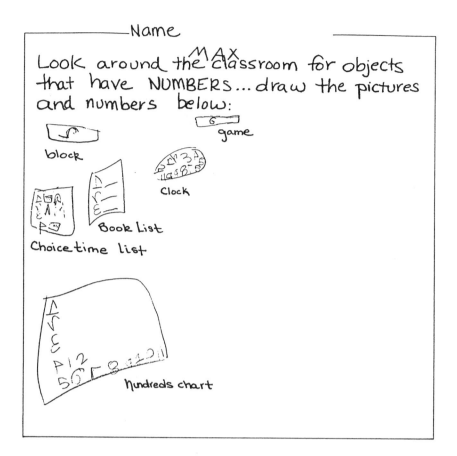

Figure 7–3. Max found these numbers in his classroom.

AT HOME: A NUMBER HUNT

Number searches in and around the school help focus the children on the many numbers in our environment. For homework, ask them to do a thorough number search in their kitchens. Younger children will probably find numbers on stoves, microwaves, clocks, and thermometers and, with some help, on measuring cups and spoons and on cans of food. (See Figures 7–4 and 7–5.) Older children may make more thorough investigations, looking inside the stove, refrigerator, and freezer, under the toaster oven, and into the food cabinets (where many numbers can be found on canned goods).

BACK IN SCHOOL: WHAT CAN I DO WITH ALL THESE NUMBERS?

Collecting numbers may be fun and instructive, but most of the learning will come from *doing something* with these numbers. Here are some suggestions:

KITCHEN NUMBERS

Figure 7–4.
Collin's kitchen
numbers.

**HELPFUL HINTS
FOR TEACHERS**

What Kinds of Things Do Kitchen Numbers Do?

The most visible numbers are those on stoves, blenders, microwaves, toaster ovens, timers, and clocks, as well as inside refrigerators and freezers. All these numbers relate to time or temperature. Numbers on measuring cups and spoons and on the inside of pots, as well as numbers on some cans and bottles, refer to volume: how many fluid ounces, pints, quarts, or liters of this liquid will fit into the container? Numbers on other cans and bottles, as well as some of the numbers on packaged foods, measure weight. Sometimes numbers on packaged foods give a count of the items in the package. All these numbers give us information about a quantity that can be measured. It's important for kids to think about the meanings of the numbers they encounter so they can begin to see how we use them in everyday activities.

Figure 7–5.
Courtney's kitchen
numbers.

Younger children

- Make a kitchen mural showing the numbers children have discovered on large objects like stoves, microwaves, clocks, and so on.
- Make a large collage from can and other wrappers sent to school by families. Highlight the numbers on the wrappers.
- Draw pictures of objects that measure time and temperature. Additional ideas may well come from the children.

Older children

- Classify the numbers by function: identifying, counting, and measuring.
- Create further measurement categories and make illustrated charts of all the objects that measure time and temperature.
- List and draw objects that measure volume, such as measuring cups and spoons, cooking pots, and plastic storage containers.
- Study the volume and weight of numbers on cans and boxes.

This section deals with numbers that identify, count, and measure. It is interesting to learn how widely numbers are used for identification purposes, but it is more important for children to understand that the specific information provided by numbers that count or measure is used constantly, by all of us, in ordinary everyday activities.

Shapes Everywhere

Every object in the world has a shape. The most commonly seen shapes have been given names—circles, squares, rectangles, cubes, cylinders, spheres, and so on. These shapes, and many more, can be seen in city and country, in things made by people and in things found in nature. Hunting for and discussing shapes helps children both to identify them and to acquire the language of geometry.

IN SCHOOL: BECOMING AWARE OF SHAPES

You can help your students become aware of all the different shapes in their environment by looking for shapes in the classroom and the building, as well as by taking a neighborhood "shape walk." Try to get some of Tana Hoban's wonderful picture books on shapes in the library. Here are a few titles (there are many more!):

Over, Under and Through, 1973 (New York: McMillan).

Circles, Triangles and Squares, 1974 (New York: McMillan).

Shapes, Shapes, Shapes, 1986 (New York: Greenwillow).

Books like these will help the children to see shapes everywhere! When they have become "shape conscious," they can continue their shape hunt at home.

AT HOME: BEING SHAPE DETECTIVES

Suggest that kids start a shape search in their kitchens. This activity can be done by children of all ages. Adapt the ideas to your students' age level and keep young children's shape hunts simple. Children may find some or all of the following shapes to bring back to school for a class display:

Round shapes
- Circles: plates and pot lids of all sizes; the rims and bottoms of pots and pans, glasses, and bowls.
- Cylinders: food cans and rolling pins, oatmeal boxes and paper towel rolls.
- Spheres: cantaloupes and grapes, apples and oranges.
- Cones: funnels and coffee filters.
- Hemispheres: strainers, colanders, rounded bowls, grapefruit halves.
- Teardrops: pears, avocados, light bulbs.

Rectangular shapes
- Squares: baking pans, cutting boards, pot holders.
- Other rectangles: some griddles, electric frying pans, cookie sheets, dish towels.
- Cubes: sugar and bouillon cubes, ice "cubes" (which aren't all cubes), tins of tea.
- Other prisms: boxes of all sizes (for cereal, crackers, raisins, sugar, dried milk, light bulbs), sticks of butter or margarine, packaged cheeses.

BACK IN SCHOOL: SORTING THE SHAPES

Display the shapes the children bring in and have them talk about what they found. Who has something with straight edges, flat sides, a curved surface, sharp points? Let the children feel the edges and corners, and note what shape names they know. Let them explore the shapes freely and see whether they start to classify them on their own. If they don't, encourage them to sort the shapes, after which you can supply the needed geometric names. Additional shapes can be searched for and added to the collection when the original batch has been sorted. When the kids have become familiar with all the different shapes, they can start a "Shape of the Week" display in the hall and invite other classes to add to it.

Young children learn best through their senses. Handling shapes, feeling round or flat sides, touching edges and corners (called "lines" and "points" in geometry), seeing which shapes roll or spin, will help them remember what the different shapes are like. Children will recall the shape names more easily if they have had these kinds of experiences.

It is also important that children see all these shapes in different sizes. A cylinder, for instance, can be a tall can of tomato juice, a squat little can of tuna fish, or any of the possible variations of height and width in between. Seeing this variety of sizes will help children remember what it is that these cans have in common, what, in fact, makes them cylindrical.

Firsthand experiences with three-dimensional kitchen shapes will provide children with a solid foundation for later work with shapes in geometry classes.

Multiplication Stories

Anything that comes in regular sets or has rows and columns can be used to introduce multiplication. Kitchens are full of such things: crackers packaged in sets, six-packs of juice, muffin tins, ice-cube trays, forks with three or four tines each, and many more. Working with these familiar objects can help children see multiplication as a shortcut for addition—an understanding as important in problem solving as being able to produce the right answer. Creating and solving such problems will help children understand what multiplication means and recognize situations in which it can be useful.

IN SCHOOL: PICTURING MULTIPLICATION

Draw attention to a few things in the classroom that comprise groups of the same size—the windows and their panes, for example. Begin a list showing how we can describe each one of these using the x symbol for "times":

Five windows, two panes in each window, ten panes ($5 \times 2 = 10$)

Two gerbils, four legs on each gerbil, eight legs ($2 \times 4 = 8$)

Two hands, five fingers on each hand, ten fingers ($2 \times 5 = 10$)

Challenge the students to add to your list.

Do some brainstorming about similar things the children know that are not in the classroom but that also contain groups of the same size. List these on the board and let each child choose one to illustrate. Rubber stamps, if you have them, are particularly appealing for making multiplication pictures, but drawings are equally effective. A description of each picture should be written underneath, just as you have modeled it on the chart.

AT HOME: MULTIPLES IN THE KITCHEN

Send home a sheet (Figure 7–6) asking parents to join the children in exploring their kitchens for objects that show groups of the same size. See how many objects they can find and ask them to list these on the sheet or draw pictures of them.

BACK IN SCHOOL: WRITING MULTIPLICATION PROBLEMS

The discoveries children have made at home will be a rich fund of information for story problems. Display all the lists and drawings so that

Figure 7–6. Worksheet to help parents explore with their children objects that are grouped in sets. (A reproducible master for this form in included in the Appendix.)

TO GET READY FOR WRITING MULTIPLICATION STORIES WE ARE LOOKING FOR OBJECTS WHICH REGULARLY COME IN SETS OF A CERTAIN SIZE. YOUR KITCHEN IS AN EXCELLENT PLACE TO FIND SUCH THINGS (LIKE FORKS WITH FOUR TINES EACH OR GRAHAM CRACKERS IN PACKAGES OF 8).

PLEASE HELP YOUR CHILD TO LOOK FOR MORE EXAMPLES AND TO NAME OR DRAW SOME OF THESE IN THE BOXES BELOW. FEEL FREE TO INCLUDE OBJECTS OR SETS FROM OTHER PARTS OF YOUR HOME AS WELL.

Tea Bags	Chewing Gum	Granola Bars
6 bags in a packet 6 packets in a box	12 pieces in a packet 24 packets in a bag	3 flavors 8 bars of each flavor
Choclate Wafers 2 rows in each packet 8 wafers in each row	Plates 8 large 8 Medium 8 small 8 bowls	Oatmeal Cookies 2 rows in each packet 4 stacks in each row 4 cookies in each stack

everyone can see the number and variety of possibilities. Model the writing of a problem by telling the children about something you found in *your* kitchen: "I found a muffin tin in my kitchen. It has four rows of cups and there are three cups in each row. How many muffins could I bake at one time in this tin?" Write out your problem as the children begin to write problems about their own pictures. Display yours as an example. When the children are finished, let them read their story problems to each other and discuss them in small groups or pairs, each group being responsible for making sure that the problems are clearly stated and can be solved with the information given. The story problems can then be written by the authors in final form, illustrated and either displayed or assembled as a book. A story problem by a third grader is shown in Figure 7–7, one by a second grader in Figure 7–8.

Figure 7–7.
Magda's multiplication story problems.

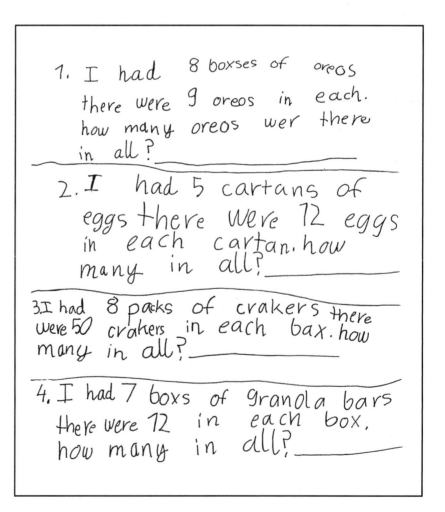

1. I had 8 boxses of oreos
there were 9 oreos in each.
how many oreos wer there
in all?

2. I had 5 cartans of
eggs there were 12 eggs
in each cartan. how
many in all?

3. I had 8 packs of crakers there
were 50 crahers in each bax. how
many in all?

4. I had 7 boxs of granola bars
there were 12 in each box,
how many in all?

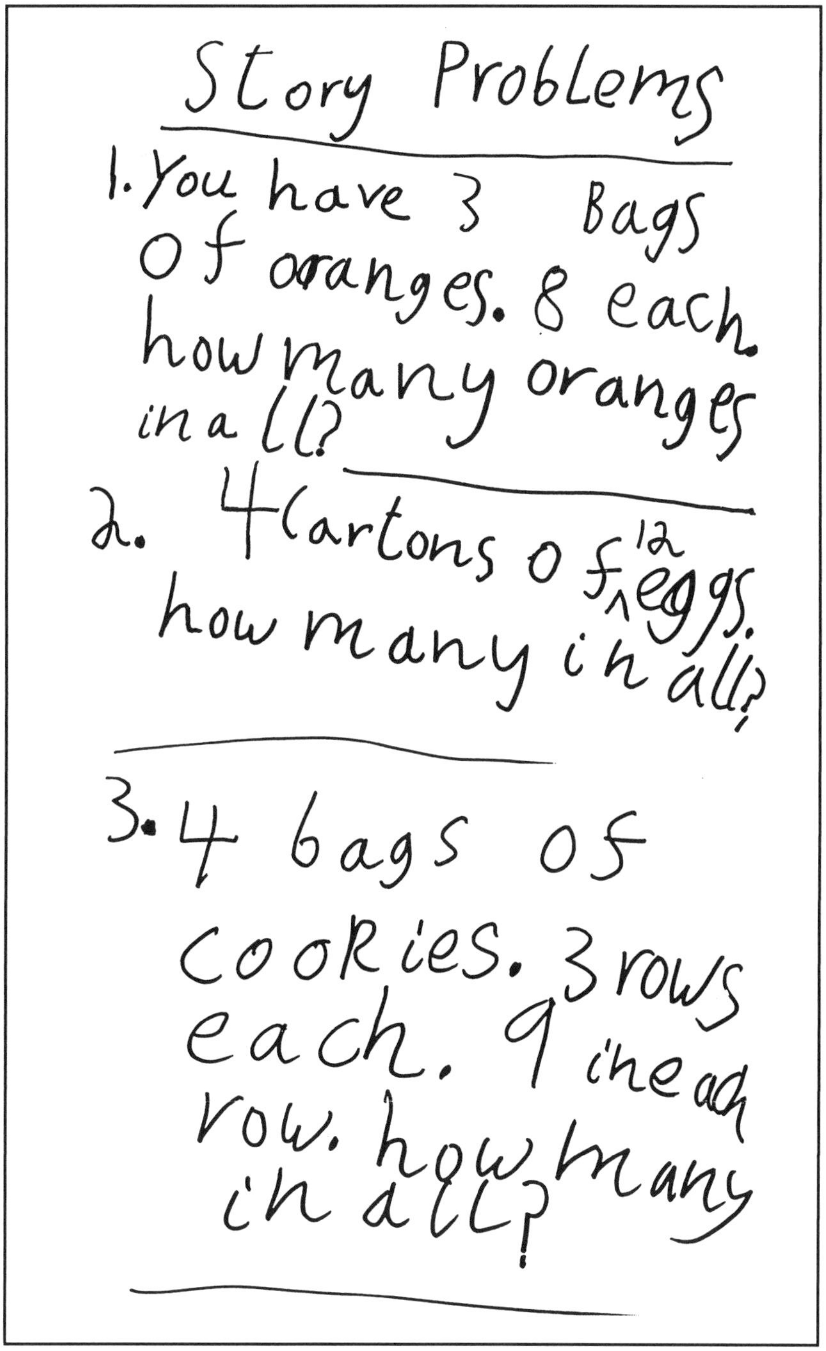

Story Problems

1. You have 3 Bags of oranges. 8 each. how many oranges in all?

2. 4 Cartons of 12 eggs. how many in all?

3. 4 bags of cookies. 3 rows each. 9 ine ach row. how many in all?

Figure 7–8.
Jenny's multiplication story problems.

Multiplication on a Larger Scale

As soon as children know what multiplication is all about and can multiply with a calculator, they can solve a variety of interesting problems. Problems about family food consumption are a good starting point. In the process of solving these problems children will discover how rapidly quantities increase when multiplied by whole numbers. They will also gain more familiarity with situations to which multiplication can be applied.

IN SCHOOL: HOW MANY EGGS DO WE EAT IN ONE YEAR?

Put on the board how many eggs, gallons of milk, and loaves of bread your own family consumes in a week. Divide the class into small groups, give each group a calculator, and challenge the students to figure out how many eggs, and so on, you would consume in a whole year. Children can solve problems like this with a calculator even if they do not yet know how to multiply large numbers with pencil and paper. (Such problems can also, of course, be solved by addition.)

Discuss the groups' answers and the strategies they used to solve the problem. Ask the class to decide which was the most efficient method and what information is needed in order to use that method (number of weeks in a year, for example).

It's fun to see your daily or weekly food consumption projected into such large numbers. Ask the students to suggest other food consumption questions. For example:

■ How many hamburgers does the local fast-food restaurant serve in a year?
■ How many sandwiches have I eaten since I was born?
■ How many half-pints of milk are sold in the school cafeteria in a month?

Questions of this nature can rarely be answered precisely. Ask the students why we might not be able to find an *exact* answer to every question. Let them choose a question to try to answer and talk about what kind of information is needed. Children may be able to supply some of this information: How many years have you been eating sandwiches? How many sandwiches do you eat in one week? Other information (How many cartons of milk are sold in the school cafeteria each day?) may have to be obtained from other sources.

Children can work on the problems in pairs or groups. The results are bound to be impressively large and could be the beginning of a display or a publication of "amazing facts."

AT HOME: FOOD CONSUMPTION

When you are sure your students understand how to solve these kinds of problems, have each of them write out a family food consumption question to solve at home, leaving blanks for the information they will need to obtain (see Figure 7–9).

Figure 7–9.
Form on which to record a family food question. (A reproducible master for this form in included in the Appendix.)

FAMILY FOOD QUESTION

How much __Milk_____ does our family eat (or <u>drink</u>) in a year?
  or
How many _____ do our family eat (or drink) in a year?

WRITE THE FOOD OR DRINK OF YOUR CHOICE IN ONE OR BOTH OF THE QUESTIONS ABOVE. TAKE YOUR QUESTION(S) HOME AND TRY TO ESTIMATE AN ANSWER WITH YOUR FAMILY. ASK OTHERS IN YOUR FAMILY FOR ANY INFORMATION YOU NEED BUT DON'T HAVE. ALSO ASK THEM HOW <u>THEY</u> WOULD ESTIMATE THE ANSWER. IT'S O.K. TO USE A CALCULATOR.

Our answer to this question is _208 gallons_.

This is how we found it:
We drink 4 gallons a week
We multiplied 4 by 52.

$$4 \times 52 = 208$$

Here are some other questions we would like to answer:

How many pizzas do we eat in 5 years if we have pizza every Saturday?

Our family chews about 3 packs of gum a month. How many packs would we chew in 2 years?

BACK IN SCHOOL: IN ONE YEAR . . .

Make a large chart on which you list all the family food consumption facts that children have brought in. Each child can write down how many eggs, oranges, cereal boxes, frozen pizzas, and so on, are consumed by his or her family in one year. If there is interest, you can also spend some time answering other questions proposed by families and add these to the display:

- How much time have I spent brushing my teeth in my lifetime?
- How much time do I spend riding the school bus in a single school year?
- If I live to be seventy, how much time am I likely to have spent watching television?

What Is One Half?

Kitchens are veritable fraction factories. There are ingredients to be measured, fruits and vegetables to be cut, and foods to be divided into equal portions. If we all used the language of fractions more consciously as we dealt with fractional parts in our daily lives, children would have a chance to gain the same kind of familiarity with halves, thirds, and fourths as they have with whole numbers.

Often children learn about fractions with certain specially designed materials like fraction bars or pie diagrams. Some children will associate a *half* or a *quarter* with the shape from which they learned these concepts. It's important that children see common fractions in many different sizes and shapes. The kitchen provides this opportunity. *Half,* for instance, can be half a grapefruit, half a loaf of bread, half an avocado, half a stick of butter, even half a dozen eggs—and all these halves look different. Children can divide things in half, handle these different halves, and then put them together again to see the original whole. These experiences will help them understand that halves can look very different, but the *idea* of one half is always the same. The same holds true for other fractions.

A teacher of first- and second-grade students sent home the note shown in Figure 7–10. Students brought in a variety of halves to share with the class. They also wanted to have a record of where in their homes they had found these halves (see Figure 7–11). There was much discussion and further work on halves after this initial project.

Figure 7–10. Lisa's note to parents.

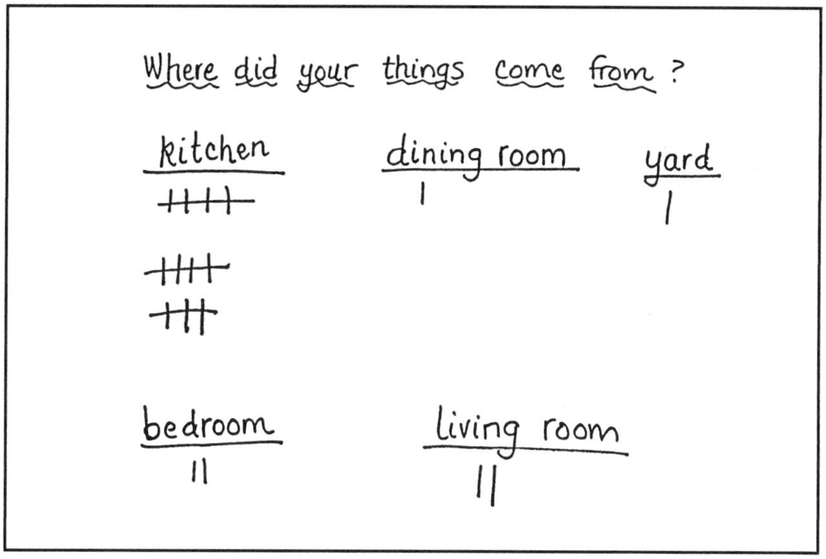

Homework

Lisa's Class   Monday December 7

cut something up!!

Parents, Thursday and Friday this week, our class will be exploring the concept of $\frac{1}{2}$. Please look around your house (kitchen particularly) and help your child find something that illustrates this. Please send in both halves in a paper bag. Thanks. Lisa

Figure 7–11. Tally chart for the halves Lisa's students brought into the classroom.

Where did your things come from?

kitchen   dining room   yard

|||| |||| | |

|||| ||||

|||

bedroom   living room

|| ||

What is one half? First and second graders display many different examples they've brought from home.

Seeing Fractions in Action

Fractions are numbers; like whole numbers, they can be added, subtracted, multiplied, and divided. The meanings of these operations for fractions, however, are not always understood. Whole-number operations can be carried out by counting or manipulating small objects. Fortunately, similar concrete methods of calculating with fractions do exist and can contribute much to children's understanding. Kitchens are full of fractions, but kids won't be frightened by them if they learn how to work with them while baking cookies or dividing their favorite kind of pie.

IN SCHOOL: INTRODUCING FRACTIONS

You can introduce operations with fractions using whatever concrete materials you normally use. The family homework part of this activity can be done at any time during this introduction or it can serve as a reminder of the meaning of fraction operations before going on to more formal paper-and-pencil work.

AT HOME: EXPERIMENTING WITH FRACTIONS

Send home the letter and series of worksheets shown in Figures 7–12 through 7–16 (pp. 126–130) or make up your own set.

BACK IN SCHOOL: FINDING OTHER FRACTION MODELS

After each family homework assignment, divide the class into groups and let group members compare their results. Then give each group a kit with which to do their work. You will need egg cartons, rulers, and real or play money—quarters, half-dollars (available at banks), and dollar bills—for the following experiments.

The first day's experiment requires eight quarters, four half-dollars, two one-dollar bills, a pencil, and some paper. Ask each group to name the coins as fractions of a dollar. Then ask them to use the coins to verify that $1/2 + 1/4 = 3/4$. What other fraction facts can they discover using the items in the kit? Make sure each group records all their facts, so they can compare results when finished.

The second day's experiment requires four twelve-inch rulers. Each group should draw line segments as long as $1/3$ of the ruler, then verify that $4 \times 1/3 = 1\frac{1}{3}$. Again, students can look for additional fraction facts.

The third day's experiment requires six egg cartons, a pair of scissors, a pencil, and a sheet of paper. Ask each group to cut one egg carton in half, two egg cartons into thirds, and two egg cartons into fourths and then use the egg cartons to verify the results of the day's experiments.

The fourth set of experiments again requires rulers. Ask the groups to work with fractions of an inch to verify their calculations.

Are there other fraction facts that can be demonstrated with the material from the kit?

Figure 7–12.
Letter to parents about learning fractions in the kitchen. (A reproducible master for this form letter in included in the Appendix.)

Dear Parents,

You may already have heard from your children that we are studying fractions. In school, we try to use phrases like "one third," "three fourths," "one and two fifths," and so on, as often as possible. It helps children to become familiar with these concepts.

We would really appreciate it if you could try to "talk fractions" with your kids whenever you are dividing up food. When cutting up a pizza, you can talk about slicing it into eighths. Some apple corers also cut apples into twelve equal sections and these can be referred to as twelfths. If four people are to share the apple, each one will get one quarter or three twelfths. Children can be asked to divide a banana into quarters, a peeled orange into fifths, or a loaf cake into sixths. Give your children time to find their own strategies for dividing different shapes; this will help them see which fractions are relatively easy to section off and which are more difficult. How do you cut a pizza into fifths or tenths?

It would also be most helpful if your kids could assist you with any measuring you have to do when preparing meals. A set of measuring spoons and cups would make a great gift when children are learning about fractions. Your children could experiment with a couple of large bowls, a set of measuring cups and spoons, and some salt or cornmeal, and gain useful practice for future measuring jobs.

Thank you so much for your cooperation.

Sincerely,

FRACTION EXPERIMENTS -- FIRST DAY

Ask someone in your family to show you the fractional markings on a one-cup measure. Ask that person to help you while you do the following:

Measure 1/4 cup of water and pour it into a glass.

Next measure 1/2 cup of water and leave it in the cup.

Pour the water from the glass back into the measuring cup.

Read the marking at the water level.

How much water is in the cup? _____

$$\frac{1}{2} + \frac{1}{4} = \underline{\hspace{1cm}}$$

Experiment with the measuring cup to find two more addition facts using fractions.

Write them here.

_____

_____

Figure 7–13.
Fraction experiments—first day. (A reproducible master for this form is included in the Appendix.)

FRACTION EXPERIMENTS -- SECOND DAY

Get out the measuring cup again. Ask someone in your family to keep count as you measure $\frac{1}{3}$ cup of water and pour it into a glass four times.

Then measure the water in the glass.

How much is there? _____

$$4 \times \frac{1}{3} = \text{_____}$$

Ask your partner to measure out $\frac{1}{4}$ cup of water 3 times. Write a new multiplication sentence to describe the result.

_____

Measure out $\frac{1}{4}$ cup of water 2 times. Write a multiplication sentence to describe the result.

_____

Figure 7–14.
Fraction experiments—second day.
(A reproducible master for this form is included in the Appendix.)

FRACTION EXPERIMENTS -- THIRD DAY

Get your measuring partner to watch while you pour $1\frac{1}{2}$ cups of water into a container. Divide the water evenly between two identical glasses. Measure the water in one glass. How much is there?

$$\frac{1}{2} \text{ of } 1\frac{1}{2} \text{ is } \underline{\hspace{1cm}}.$$

Write $\frac{1}{2} \times 1\frac{1}{2} = \underline{\hspace{1cm}}$

Now watch while your partner does the same thing, starting with $\frac{2}{3}$ cup of water.

$$\frac{1}{2} \times \frac{2}{3} = \underline{\hspace{2cm}}$$

Do it once more, starting with $1\frac{1}{3}$ cups of water.

$$\frac{1}{2} \times 1\frac{1}{3} = \underline{\hspace{1.5cm}}$$

Figure 7–15.
Fraction experiments—third day. (A reproducible master for this form is included in the Appendix.)

FRACTION EXPERIMENTS -- FOURTH DAY

Cut an apple, a pizza, or something else you are eating into eight equal pieces. Eat one of the eighths.

How many eighths are left? _____.

$$1 - \frac{1}{8} = \text{\_\_\_\_\_}$$

Put six of the remaining $\frac{1}{8}$ pieces on a plate and let two members of your family take one apiece. Ask them to guess what fraction of the whole will be left.

What fraction <u>is</u> left on the plate? _____

$$\frac{6}{8} - \frac{2}{8} = \text{\_\_\_\_\_}$$

Do you have enough of the eighths left over to make one half? _____

If so, how many eighths did it take to make the half? _____

$$\frac{1}{2} \div \frac{1}{8} = \text{\_\_\_\_\_}$$

Milk Cartons and Powers of Two

Milk cartons from home and from the cafeteria make excellent containers for studying doubling or the powers of two. In the United States milk is sold in cartons of different sizes:

Half-pint.........................	1 cup or	8 ounces
Pint	2 cups or	16 ounces
Quart...........................	4 cups or	32 ounces
Half-gallon......... 2 quarts or ...	8 cups or	64 ounces
Gallon .... 4 quarts or ...	16 cups or	128 ounces

Figuring out these relationships by themselves gives children an experience on which to base conversions from one unit of measure to another. It also offers an introduction to a new subject: exponential growth.

Gather a complete set of milk cartons from home, from the cafeteria, and if necessary, from the supermarket. Cut off the tops of the cartons where they are folded. Fill each carton with the amount of water it is supposed to hold. If this amount does not fill the carton, mark the water level on the inside of the carton. Also provide several measuring cups with spouts for pouring.

Younger children can use a cup measure to pour water into the larger containers to find out how many cups are needed to fill each one to the line. Use the recording sheet shown in Figure 7–17 and let the children choose whether to keep track by tally or by writing down the numbers. Talk about the measurements they have found. Ask whether they see any patterns in the numbers.

Older children can weigh the filled cartons as well as measure them in cups. They can then prepare a similar table that includes both volume and weight measurements.

If students are familiar with exponents, you can ask them to use these to describe the patterns in the numbers of cups and ounces. If they are not, this is a good time to introduce them to exponents to express powers of 2:

$$4 = 2 \times 2 = 2^2$$
$$8 = 2 \times 2 \times 2 = 2^3$$
$$16 = 2 \times 2 \times 2 \times 2 = 2^4$$

Figure 7–16.
(*Opposite*) Fraction experiments—fourth day. (A reproducible master for this form is included in the Appendix.)

The three smallest sizes of milk cartons—half-pint, pint, and quart—provide a good visual demonstration of the fact that volume can be doubled by doubling only one dimension. Students can compare the widths, depths, and heights of these three containers. Which dimensions stay the same? Which ones change? Students who are interested can explore how much the pint container would hold if two or all

HOW MANY CUPS?

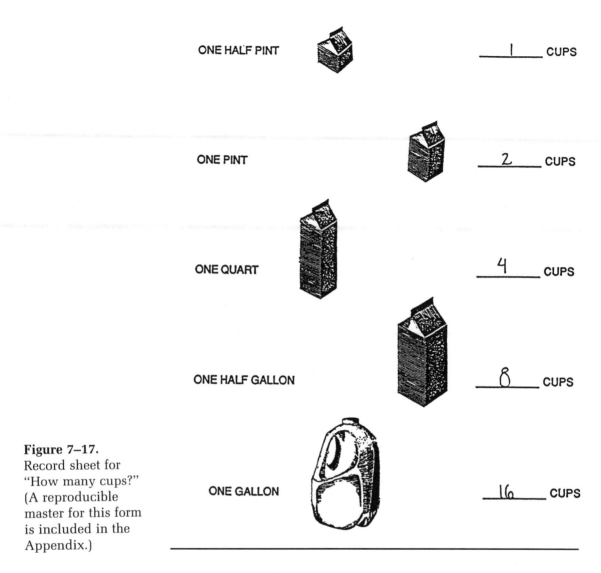

ONE HALF PINT   _____1_____ CUPS

ONE PINT   _____2_____ CUPS

ONE QUART   _____4_____ CUPS

ONE HALF GALLON   _____8_____ CUPS

ONE GALLON   _____16_____ CUPS

Figure 7–17.
Record sheet for
"How many cups?"
(A reproducible
master for this form
is included in the
Appendix.)

three dimensions of the half-pint carton were doubled instead of just the height.

Twice as Much Cake

Most of us alter recipes occasionally when we wish to make more or less than the amount given in cookbooks. Increasing or decreasing ingredients in a recipe can raise interesting mathematical problems that can be as puzzling to adults as to children.

IN SCHOOL: DOUBLING THE VOLUME

To get this project started, give the children some flour, salt, and colored water to make play dough. (Though they may not admit it, even upper elementary kids enjoy making dough and messing around with it.) Here is a simple recipe:

PLAY DOUGH

$^1/_2$ cup salt
1 cup flour
Approximately $^2/_3$ cup of colored water.

    Knead to a proper consistency. (Some people add a few drops of oil for smoothness.)

Have the kids make enough play dough so that four to six children can work with it at one time. After some initial exploratory play, divide up the play dough so that each student can have three balls of equal size.

First have each student take one ball and create a shape or sculpture. Next, ask each student to combine the two remaining lumps of dough and make the same shape or sculpture. The second sculpture has twice as much volume as the first one: does it look twice as big?

When all the students have had a chance to work with the play dough, ask them to share questions and discoveries in a group discussion. There is no need to come to a conclusion at this time.

AT HOME: DOUBLING A RECIPE

Send home a recipe, and a letter to parents explaining this project. (A brief letter to parents and a sample assignment are shown in Figures 7–18 and 7–19.) If you send your own recipe, make sure it contains a recommended pan size, baking temperature, and baking time as well as measurements of ingredients.

BACK IN SCHOOL: COMPARING RESULTS

When the assignment is finished, have small groups of students compare and discuss their revised recipes and taste the samples brought to school. Here are some questions to ask:

Figure 7–18.
Letter to parents about doubling a recipe. (A reproducible master for this form letter is included in the Appendix.)

Dear Parents,

Kitchen-related mathematics seems to have no end! We've been wondering what happens when you double a bread or cake recipe. Each student will bring home a copy of the same recipe. However, since we like variety, feel free to substitute your own favorite bread or cake recipe for this experiment. It will make our tasting party more interesting.

Please help your child when necessary but let him or her try to figure out what to do even if you know that the result may not be perfect. We all learn from our mistakes! Thanks for your help and your patience.

Sincerely,

Figure 7–19.
Instructions and recipe for the doubling assignment. (A reproducible master for this assignment is included in the Appendix.)

The following recipe serves four people. Double it, so that it will serve eight. Please write out the entire new recipe, including the size of pan you used, oven temperature, and baking time. Ask someone in your family to be available to help you with this project.

Please do this assignment by _____ and, if possible, bring a sample of your baking to school.

CORN BREAD

Sift these together:

³/₄ cup cornmeal	2 tablespoons sugar
¹/₂ cup flour	¹/₄ teaspoon salt
2 teaspoons baking powder	

Combine these and beat them:

1 egg	2 tablespoons melted
¹/₂ cup milk	margarine

Now do this:

Turn on the oven and set it to 425 degrees

Grease a loaf pan (9″ x 4″)

Combine the two mixtures, stir until they are well blended, and pour them into the greased pan.

Bake the mixture for 20 to 25 minutes.

- Have *all* the numbers in the recipes been doubled?
- What happens to the baking time if you double the ingredients of a cake? Did you double it or adjust it?
- How do you decide on the size of a pan if you have doubled the ingredients?
- Did you look for a pan that was twice as big? Twice as big in which way?
- Did you think about doubling the oven temperature?

Perhaps the most confusing change that has to be made is the selection of the right-sized pan. If you take a round pan that has twice the diameter of the original, you can tell immediately by looking at it that it is much too large. If you have baking facilities in your classroom or access to the stove in your school kitchen, your students could do some further testing of the doubled recipe. Let them agree what needs doubling and what needs adjusting, and be prepared for several revisions before you get the correct results. Students will learn a lot by the mistakes they may make.

Halving a recipe can be the next step in this baking project. It will be interesting to see whether children can apply their learning from the doubling experiments.

How Much Does This Cup Hold? Estimating Volume

Becoming a good judge of volume takes a lot of experience. Pouring water from one container to another is a favorite activity of preschool and kindergarten children. It is the way young children build up experiences that become the foundation for their later learning. Older students also benefit from exploratory work with a variety of containers before they proceed to more formal measuring. This kind of "messing around" plays an important role in children's learning.

IN SCHOOL: FREE EXPERIMENTATION

Experiences with estimating volume can familiarize students with common units of measure and help them make good judgments of quantity. After setting up a protected area for "water play" in the

First graders "mess around" with water.

classroom and equipping it with many different sizes and shapes of containers, provide time for the children to experiment with pouring, filling containers, estimating sizes, and so on. After this exploratory experience, students will be ready for the following home experiment.

AT HOME: VOLUME EXPERIMENT

Give your students the assignment shown in Figure 7–20 to take home, and encourage their parents to participate.

HELPFUL HINTS FOR TEACHERS

> ### *Understanding Invariance*
>
> When children are misled by appearances in their judgment of volume, it means they have not yet developed an understanding of "conservation" or "invariance." Young children believe that a tall container, even if quite narrow, will hold more water than a shorter and wider one. Adults often make similar mistakes when dealing with unfamiliar shapes. The understanding of invariance develops gradually—it cannot be hurried or taught. (Also see "Conservation" in Chapter 2.)

BACK IN SCHOOL: MORE VOLUME EXPERIMENTS

When everyone has completed the assignment, call the students together for a discussion and have them share their experiences. If they would like to repeat this experiment in school, ask each student to bring some of the containers used at home. There should be enough containers for three or four pairs of children to work at a time. Be sure you have quart and liter containers for each pair so that kids can gain experience with these measurements. You will have to renumber the containers. Numbering each group's set with a different-colored marking pen will help to keep the collections separate.

In addition to improving the ability to judge comparative volume, such experiences help students to gain a good sense of the relative sizes of standard units such as liters and quarts. A feeling for volume, based on firsthand experiences, makes later formal computations and conversions much easier.

Gathering and Preparing Materials

Collect an assortment of bottles, bowls, and plastic food and storage containers from your kitchen.

Remove or cover all labels on the containers so that the measurements cannot be seen.

Add a funnel to the collection to help you with pouring liquids.

Doing the Experiment - Part I

Line up all the containers by increasing volume: Start with the one that you think will hold the least amount of liquid and continue lining up containers until you get to the one that you think will hold the most.

Number the containers in order from the one you think is smallest to the one you think is largest.

Doing the Experiment - Part II

For the second part of the experiment you need a pitcher of water with a few drops of food coloring in it. This will make it easier to see the water level if you are using transparent containers.

Try to establish the true order of volume of your containers—from the smallest to the largest one—by pouring water from one to the other.

Compare the new order with your estimated order.

Describe your results in writing: How correct were your estimates when you lined up all the containers by increasing volume?

Try to figure out where a quart—and if possible a liter—fit into the sequence.

Were there any surprises when you started to measure the containers? Did some of the shapes of bottles or containers mislead you?

Did you observe anything that might improve your future volume estimates?

Do you have questions or discoveries to share with the class?

Figure 7–20.
A volume experiment to do at home. (A reproducible master for this assignment is included in the Appendix.)

This chapter offers a long list of kitchen activities, all filled with mathematical content. From simple matching and counting for the youngest children to the more sophisticated tasks of doubling recipes and estimating volume for older students, the kitchen offers both teachers and parents a wealth of opportunities to link mathematics to children's natural love of food and cooking.

8
Eating Out

Restaurants abound with opportunities for mathematical calculations: Can we afford to eat at this restaurant? Is it more expensive to order à la carte? How much should we leave as a tip?

The economics of the restaurant business, of prime interest to owners, employees, and managers, can also be of interest to customers. Why are fast-food establishments less expensive than more formal eateries? How many people can be served in a given restaurant at one time? How much food should be prepared on a given day? How much does a waiter or waitress earn in tips?

As children and their families explore questions like these, they will become more conscious of everyday mathematics. At the same time, they will have opportunities to use their mathematical skills in computing, estimating, dealing with ratio and proportion, calculating volume and area, and gathering and analyzing the data needed to make informed decisions. Children will also be introduced to new career opportunities and the economics of the marketplace. Some of the questions you raise in school may become topics of conversation for families while they are standing in line at a restaurant or waiting for their meals to be served.

Comparing Capacities of Beverage Containers

Restaurant beverages are obtainable in many different sizes, with and without ice. Which are the best buys? How does the cost compare with beverages you buy in the supermarket or prepare yourself and serve at home? The answers may help both children and adults to make choices.

IN SCHOOL:
MEASURING VOLUME AND COMPUTING COST

Begin by visiting a local fast-food restaurant yourself to collect samples of the small, medium, and large containers in which beverages are served. (Get at least two of each kind.) Note the prices of soft drinks and milk sold in these containers.

When you present your containers in the classroom, make an informal survey of favorite beverages. Get your students to think about the factors that go into choosing the size (thirst, price, occasion, etc.) by asking, If each of these containers held your favorite drink, what size would you buy? Why? Acknowledge considerations other than price, but tell the children you are going to concentrate on which size would be the best buy.

Ask the children to decide to what level they think the containers should be filled and draw lines at that level. Provide ice cubes or crushed ice so they can fill the containers to the line with ice before pouring in water (or juice, if it's snack time). Then have them pour off the liquid into an identical container to see how much they would really have to drink. Would they order a drink with ice? Just a little ice? No ice? Older children may be interested in investigating whether shaved ice and ice cubes take up different amounts of space.

Next ask for ideas about how to compare the amounts of liquid (without ice) different sizes of containers could hold. Young children can simply pour the contents of one container into another one, using the smallest as the measure with which to evaluate each of the larger containers. They could also use a nonstandard unit such as a small drinking cup to measure each container. Older children can use a measuring cup to determine the number of fluid ounces each container will hold when filled to the line. Restaurants, in fact, sometimes indicate the capacity in fluid ounces on their menus or price charts.

HELPFUL HINTS FOR TEACHERS

What Are Fluid Ounces?

The difference between *fluid ounces,* which are a measure of volume, and *ounces,* which measure weight, is not widely understood. The "ounces" marked on a measuring cup are actually fluid ounces. If the cup is filled with water, these marks do indicate the weight in ounces, since a fluid ounce is the *amount* of water that weighs one ounce. This is not necessarily true for other substances. If the cup is filled with oil to a certain mark (say, eight "ounces"), the oil will not actually weigh eight ounces.

Using a sensitive balance or scale, your students may find it interesting to weigh eight fluid ounces of different substances. Those that weigh the most have the greatest *density.* Exploring which substances are more or less dense than water is a good activity for a science project.

Your class can also discuss how to compare the costs of beverages in different-sized cups. Although the standard method of comparison is to compute the cost per fluid ounce (dividing the cost by the number of fluid ounces), students may come up with methods that are equally valid: counting the number of small containers needed to fill a larger one, or counting the number of sips in each size and computing the cost per sip. Discuss the methods the children have chosen. Suggest making a chart to organize and display this information so that it is easier to compare the costs.

AT HOME: GATHERING MORE INFORMATION

The restaurant from which you obtained containers may not be the one most often patronized by your students and their families. You can ask young children to save disposable beverage containers the next time their family visits their favorite restaurant and to bring the containers to school. For older children, send home the form shown in Figure 8–1, which their families can use to record information from one of their preferred eating places: the sizes of cups available there, the number of fluid ounces they hold, the price of each size for the beverage they usually drink. Children who feel comfortable with the

Figure 8–1. Chart comparing soft drink costs. (A reproducible master for this form is included in the Appendix.)

COST OF SOFT DRINKS

AT RESTAURANTS IN ___Boulder___
(YOUR CITY OR TOWN)

RESTAURANT	SIZE	FLUID OUNCES	COST	COST PER FL. OZ
Wendy's	Sm	16 oz	75¢	4.69¢
	Med.	20 oz	95¢	4.07¢
	Large	32 oz	99¢	3.09¢
Toco Bell	Sm	16 oz	69¢	4.31¢
	Med.	20 oz	79¢	3.95¢
	Large	32 oz	99¢	3.09¢

process of comparison you used in school can repeat this at home with their parents, using the containers or information they have gathered.

BACK IN SCHOOL: COMPARING RESTAURANTS

When the results come in, organize groups according to the beverages for which they have collected information (soft drinks, milk, iced tea, whatever). Groups can compute costs, if this has not already been done, and summarize the information, by restaurant, in a table. As a class, study the tables to determine which restaurant offers the best buys in beverages. If you want to take this project further, you could purchase soft drinks or milk at the supermarket and let the students compute and add to the table the costs of providing one's own beverage. To conclude this market study, students can write reports to their parents on the results of their findings. Perhaps these will influence family decisions on where to eat.

Here are some additional questions for discussion and investigation:

- If the largest size costs less per fluid ounce, does it always make sense to buy drinks in large containers?
- Why do beverages cost more at a restaurant than they would if you bought them at the supermarket?
- How does the cost of milk in the school cafeteria compare with the cost in the supermarket or at particular restaurants? Why is there a difference?
- How much do soft drinks from vending machine cost? Is this more or less than you would pay at your favorite restaurant?

Geometry in a Restaurant Kitchen

Venturing into a restaurant kitchen is, in some ways, like entering the land of the giants. Here children will see the familiar shapes of pots, utensils, and food containers in sizes much larger than the kitchen equipment they see at home. The mathematical concept of *similar figures*—objects that have the same shape but may have different sizes—is strikingly illustrated here.

IN SCHOOL: SIZE AND SCALE OF KITCHEN UTENSILS

Talk to a restaurant manager and ask whether you could bring your children to see the kitchen at a convenient hour. In case you can't find a nearby restaurant that welcomes school groups, a visit to your own school cafeteria can be just as informative if hot meals are prepared there.

Before you go, discuss with the children what they expect to see and what they would like to find out. Make a list of the questions they want to ask. If the question of size does not come up, you can ask what they think the cooking utensils will look like.

To help children anticipate what they might see in a restaurant kitchen, you can make a display of some regular-sized cups, plates, flatware, and pots and pans and some doll-sized utensils (available in kindergarten or preschool classrooms). Ask the children what size pot they would use to cook spaghetti for a family of five, and what size would be right to prepare a spaghetti dinner for four dolls. What size pots would an Italian restaurant need to prepare sixty spaghetti dinners each night? Perhaps a family has a commercial-sized pot that could be added to the collection for a few days. With this kind of trip preparation, children will be more aware of what to look for.

First graders on a trip to a brick factory measure themselves against the giant wheels of a front-end loader.

After the visit, talk about the cooking equipment the children have seen. Which were larger than what they have at home? Which were not? Why do they think some utensils were the same size as the ones used at home? Have they ever seen other giant versions of ordinary objects? Where? What about miniature objects?

AT HOME:
LOOKING FOR LARGE AND SMALL OBJECTS

If children have shown an interest in the different sizes of kitchen utensils, they can (with their parents' help) search their homes for further examples. For instance:

- Toy cars and trucks, which they can compare with regular-sized vehicles.
- A toy plane, compared with a small passenger aircraft and a huge commercial airliner.
- Doll house furniture, child-sized tables and chairs, regular-sized furniture.

Looking for examples of things that come in very different sizes will help children to build intuitive notions of scale.

BACK IN SCHOOL: TALKING ABOUT WHY

Add the things children bring in to your display. It would be nice to have a sampling of the many wonderful children's books dealing with scale, so that children can read some of them or have them read. You can start off with the following:

Arabella, the Smallest Girl in the World, by Mem Fox, 1986 (Gosford, NSW: Ashton Scholastic).

The Biggest Cake in the World, by Joy Cowley, 1985 (Nashville, TN: Nelson).

The Borrowers, by Mary Norton, 1990 (New York: Harcourt Brace Jovanovich).

Jim and the Beanstalk, by Raymond Briggs, 1989 (New York: Putnam).

Stuart Little, by E. B. White, 1945 (New York: HarperCollins).

Menus and Bills

Many restaurants will let you have menus if you ask for them, especially if you explain why you want them. Make a collection of these for your classroom. Real menus are always more intriguing than word problems or simulations. Studying menus gives children a realistic sense of the costs of eating out, and the menus contain all the information needed to solve the countless problems the children themselves can create.

IN SCHOOL: MATH FROM MENUS

Ask the children first to plan meals they would like to eat and then to compute the cost of each meal. Let them use real restaurant order forms, if you can obtain them (many office-supply stores carry them), to list their selections.

In a primary classroom, you can set up a restaurant corner where children can play customer, waiter, or cashier using the menus you collected, a pad of order forms, and a calculator. You may even want to provide paper plates and let the children simulate the food and serve the orders.

If you are working with older students who are familiar with percentages, they can, after they determine the cost of a meal, also compute the tax and the tip. Deciding on the amount to leave as a tip is an occasion to initiate a discussion of whether a tip is appropriate at particular restaurant, how much is customary, and how percentages can be estimated. Fast-food places do not require a tip. The customary 15 percent tip can be quickly estimated by computing 10 percent (dividing by ten, which is easy) and then adding on half of that amount. Some meal taxes are easy to estimate, too. Seven percent is about half of a 15 percent tip. Five percent is half of 10 percent. A 5 percent tax plus a 15 percent tip would amount to 20 percent of the cost of the meal (10 percent doubled). Your students may suggest other methods. If you place a limit on what each student can spend, part of the process of making a choice from the menu will be to estimate the total cost, including tax and tip.

AT HOME: FAMILY ORDERS

Give each child a copy of his or her favorite menu to take home, along with a blank order form. There, the child can become waiter and cashier, taking orders from family members and computing the bills. Older students can take copies of menus from two or more restaurants so that they and their families can compare the costs of eating at these restaurants.

BACK IN SCHOOL: PLANNING A RESTAURANT TRIP

When students have had some experience in school and at home with computing the costs of meals from menus, divide the class into small groups, give each group a budget, and ask the students to plan a meal for the group that fits within that budget. Include the tip (and the tax, if your state has one). A nice conclusion to this project, if it's possible, is to plan a class trip to a restaurant for lunch, having first had the students choose orders, figure out how much will be needed to pay for them, and decide how they will raise the money.

ADDITIONAL SUGGESTIONS FOR FAMILIES

- Ask the children to total up the cost from the menu when the family goes out to eat, then compare their results with the check.
- When eating out in a restaurant, ask each member of the family to estimate how much the meal will cost. One child can use a calculator to find out whose estimate was closest.
- Collect menus. Set a price limit and ask children to decide which restaurant they would like to eat at and what they will order.

Pizza Mathematics: Area and Cost

As pizza lovers know, a large round pizza provides quite a bit more eating than a small one, in spite of the relatively small difference in their diameters. Diameters do not tell the whole story: the amount of pizza is determined by its *area*.

IN SCHOOL: COMPARING PIZZA SIZES

The tastiest and most realistic way to initiate this activity is to make real pizza in the classroom. Buy small and large pizza shells, pizza sauce, and shredded mozzarella cheese if you don't want to make the pizza from scratch, although making the toppings and stretching the dough are good experiences in measuring and in judging volume and area. Form groups to top the pizzas with pepperoni, green pepper, or mushrooms. Each group should put the same topping on both a small and a large pizza, trying to put the pieces of topping as close together as possible without overlapping. Before baking, students should count the pieces of topping on the two pizzas to compare their sizes. Finely cut toppings like green pepper can be counted more easily if groups of ten are marked off.

Does the large pizza have more, less, or just about twice as many pieces of topping as the small pizza? Is the result the same for each type of topping? Older students can compute the ratio of topping pieces on the large size to topping pieces on the small size. Are the ratios approximately the same for all groups? Would you have more to eat if you bought one large pizza or two small ones?

If it isn't practical to make real pizza, see whether a pizza parlor will give or sell you two different sizes of the cardboard discs on which pizzas are placed. Children can cover these with small paper discs or round counters to simulate pepperoni, use large beans for imitation mushrooms and green paper strips for green pepper. Again, they should count the pieces of the "topping" to compare sizes.

Students could also compare the quantities of topping in some other way, such as spreading discs, beans, and paper strips on graph paper in a rectangular shape. By counting the number of squares covered by these objects, they will be able to get comparative area measurements.

There are still other means of comparing areas. One fifth-grade class concluded that a large pizza was about twice the size of a small one simply by counting the number of slices into which they had been cut at the pizza parlor—sixteen and eight. Slices of the two seemed to provide just about the same amount to eat, even though they were shaped differently.

If your students are familiar with the use of standard units of measure for area, they can verify the results of the pizza-making experiment by drawing ten- and fourteen-inch circles (standard pizza sizes) on one-inch graph paper and then counting the number of squares in each circle. Ask the students to decide how to count the partial squares inside the circles. Students who know the formula for the area of a circle can verify the results by using the formula to compute the areas more precisely. No matter which method is used, the results are likely to be surprising. A ten-inch pizza has a radius of five inches and a fourteen-inch pizza has a radius of seven inches. Using the formula $A = \pi r^2$, we discover that their areas are:

Ten-inch pizza: $3.14 \times 5 \times 5 = 78.5$ square inches

Fourteen-inch pizza: $3.14 \times 7 \times 7 = 153.86$ square inches

The area of the large pizza is almost twice the area of the smaller pizza!

AT HOME: FAMILY FAVORITES

Ask your students to poll members of their family to find out which pizza parlor or brand is their favorite and then find out the sizes available and the cost of each size. (They can use the chart shown in Figure 8–2.) If the whole family cannot agree on a pizza parlor or

FAMILY PIZZA FAVORITES

Our family likes ___Abos_____'s pizza.

This pizza is available in the following sizes:

	SIZE	DIAMETER	COST
	Small	12"	5.65
	Large	16"	9.70
	X Large	18"	11.50

Figure 8–2. Pizza comparison chart. (A reproducible master for this form is included in the Appendix.)

brand, the student should choose the one preferred by most. In case of a tie, the student can cast the deciding vote.

BACK IN SCHOOL: THE BEST BUYS IN PIZZA

With the information they have brought from home about family favorites, students who have data from the same restaurant or brand can get together to compare costs. There are many questions to consider:

- Do some "large" (or "small") pizzas have different areas than other "large" (or "small") pizzas?
- What is the cost per square inch of each size?
- If one pizza is twice as large as another, does it cost twice as much? More or less than twice as much? How many times as much? What percentage of the smaller pizza's price?
- What is the cost per slice of the small and large pizzas? Are the slices the same size?
- Do some pizza parlors in your neighborhood make square or rectangular pizzas? How do the sizes and costs compare with those of round pizzas?

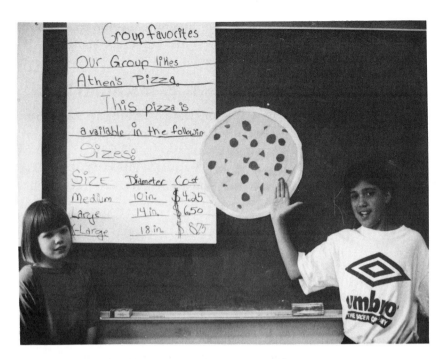

What's your favorite pizza?

Dividing up a pizza.

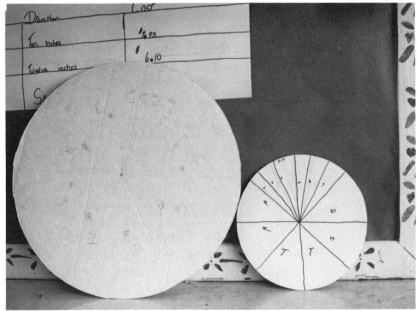

The results of this investigation can be written up by your class and published as a pizza guide for families.

ADDITIONAL PIZZA ACTIVITIES

- Explore ways of cutting a pizza into eight or sixteen equal slices or into six or twelve equal slices. How would you cut five or seven equal slices?
- If a pizza comes already cut into eight slices, how can three people share it equally? How does your family share a pizza?

Playing with Numbers

Standing in line to order or waiting for food to arrive in a restaurant needn't be dull. Parents usually appreciate suggestions about how to fill time like this profitably and enjoyably. There are many things to speculate about in a restaurant, and if suggestions come from the children themselves, all the better.

IN SCHOOL: BRAINSTORMING AND INVESTIGATING

One way to start ideas whirring is to read some statistics to your class from *In One Day* (Parker 1984). Brainstorm with your students some "in one day" questions appropriate for restaurants. For instance:

- How many french fries does a particular restaurant serve in one day?
- How many people visit the restaurant in one day?
- How many gallons of cola are served each day?
- How much does a waitress earn in tips in one day?

Encourage the students to choose one of their own questions to investigate. Talk about some of the things you would have to know in order to arrive at an approximate answer. If you want to know how many french fries are served in one day, for example, you would need to determine or estimate how many french fries there are in an order, how many people buy french fries in an hour, how many hours a day the restaurant is open, and so on.

Then divide the class into small groups. Ask each group to "invent" a restaurant, name it, and then decide on some reasonable numbers to use to answer the questions they have posed. For instance, if a group is trying to estimate the number of french fries served in one business day, they might decide that there are thirty french fries in an order, twenty-five orders purchased per hour, and ten hours in which the restaurant is open. When groups have arrived at estimates, their results can be presented as posters displaying a picture of the restaurant, the "data" they have decided to use, the estimate they have made, and a description of how the group arrived at this answer. Let each group present its method of solution and say why its members believe their estimate is reasonable.

AT HOME: FURTHER INVESTIGATIONS

Send home the list of restaurant questions the class has generated. Ask the family to choose one of these questions or come up with a question of their own to speculate about the next time they visit a restaurant. Your students may want to use the same question they investigated in class, only this time in a real restaurant setting. Stress that everyone's ideas will be welcome, but that the student will be responsible for writing down the family's question, its answer, and how the answer was arrived at. Post the students' reports as they are returned to school.

BACK IN SCHOOL: MAKING A BOOK

Family questions and estimates could become the beginning of a book entitled *One Day at a Restaurant*. Organize small groups so that the children can present their reports to one another for feedback on mathematical accuracy and reasonableness as well as for literary editing. If interest in speculating and estimating is high, the book needn't be limited to restaurants—it can be expanded to include any other questions that children have raised and answered by estimation.

Activities like these are only the beginning of exploring the mathematics of eating out. Perhaps some of your students' parents work in the restaurant business and can share mathematical questions that arise in their work. Maybe your class would like to run its own restaurant on a small scale. (See Chapter 7, "A Minitheme Involving Lots of Math and All the Children," in *Learning and Loving It*, Gamberg, et al. 1988.) If this seems like too big a project, your students can experience the challenges of setting up a food business via computer with a program like "The Lemonade Stand" from *The Marketplace* (MECC 1984).

Chapter 9   Money Management

9
Money Management

Teaching children about money is a responsibility parents and teachers can share. Parental teaching can lighten the school's load, while activities in school can complement, support, and extend what children are learning in their dealings with money at home. There is no more appropriate way to learn about money than through the everyday transactions that occur in a family setting. Instead of inventing situations in school to simulate those that occur naturally at home, it makes more sense to build family experiences into the curriculum.

Learning About Coins

To young children "money" means coins. The values we place on coins are meaningless to very young children. Coins fascinate them because of their brightness, their heft, and the idea that they can buy things. Pennies are often more highly prized than dimes simply because they are a little bit larger.

When you think about it, children are quite wise in their assessment. Although the values of coins were once based on their metallic worth, those values are now arbitrary—a matter of history and convention. There is no way to "see" the ten pennies in a dime. The materials they are made of are not equivalent in value. Since this is true, children cannot discover the values of coins on their own.

IN SCHOOL: COIN GAMES

In a kindergarten or first-grade classroom there will be some children who already know the names of coins and their values and some who do not. Simple games provide a context in which children who have yet to learn these things can do so while the others practice their skills. The games can easily be varied to fit the level of understanding of the children playing. The following two games help children learn which coin is which and how much each is worth.

155

FOUND A COIN

Preparation: Put five of each coin in a cloth or paper bag. Make four playing boards by tracing around each kind of coin and writing the name of the coin underneath the tracing.

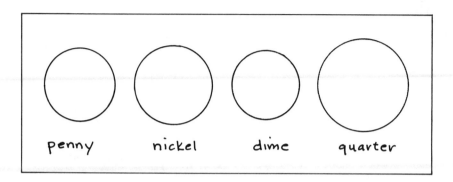

To play: Three or four players, in turn, reach into the bag and, without looking, pull out a coin. When a coin has been drawn the player announces it by saying: "I was _____*[doing something]*_____ when I found a _*[coin]*_." For example, "I was running to catch the bus when I found a dime," or "I was riding my bike when I found a quarter." The coin is then placed in the appropriate spot on the player's card. Children who aren't sure which coin they have drawn can look for the appropriate circle before naming it. Coins drawn more than once should be stacked. The winner is the first player to fill every space on his or her card. If you want to play cooperatively instead of competitively, let children who draw coins they already have give them to someone who needs one, the object being to fill all the boards.

TRADING COINS

Preparation: Number a spinner, a cube, or a set of cards using the numbers 1, 2, and 3. Provide a "cash box" containing five pennies, five nickels, and one quarter for each player, plus three extra pennies and nickels.

To play: Each player, in turn, spins, rolls the die, or draws a card and takes the indicated number of pennies. Five pennies may be traded for a nickel, and five nickels for a quarter. The first player to acquire a quarter is the winner. To play cooperatively instead of competitively, players who already have quarters should give their pennies to those who don't, the object being for everyone to get a quarter.

Extensions: It is easy to increase the challenge by adding dimes, half-dollars, and even dollar bills. Adding dimes allows the children to trade two nickels for a dime and either five nickels or two dimes and a nickel for a quarter. Adding other coins requires similar changes in the rules. If you add half-dollars and dollars, also increase the numbers on the spinner, die, or cards—to go from 1 to 6—so the game will not take too long to play. (Children can simulate bills if you give them dollar-sized pieces of green paper.)

Variation: Once the target is reached, trade down, giving back the number of pennies indicated by the spin, roll, or draw.

AT HOME: TEACHING THE GAMES TO OTHERS

Have each child make the equipment needed for one or both games— the playing boards for "Found a Coin" and the spinner, cube, or cards for "Trading Coins." They can then take these home and teach their family members to play. Don't send along photocopied directions: let the children explain how to play. It will give them good experience in communicating clearly and sequentially. You can start them thinking about what to say by asking volunteers to explain the game in class, then asking what the children thought was especially effective about each child's explanation.

BACK IN SCHOOL: COINS TO SPEND

Ask the children how many pennies you could get for a dime. Let them experiment by trading backward if necessary. Write the value of a dime as 10¢. Then ask whether there is any other combination of coins worth a dime. Record all the different combinations and continue with other coins they have been using. With the children, make a chart showing the value of each coin and all the different combinations of other coins that could be traded for it.

Set up a store in a corner of the room using small items the children donate. Have them make price labels showing prices corresponding to the coins they have been using in the trading game: 1¢, 5¢, 10¢, 25¢, 50¢, and $1, or a subset of these. Provide a change purse stocked with play money for the customer, and a cash box for the storekeeper. Children can take turns buying and selling.

Counting Change

If children have practiced making change for individual coins, it's a short step for them to determine the value of a collection of coins. There are many opportunities for practicing this skill.

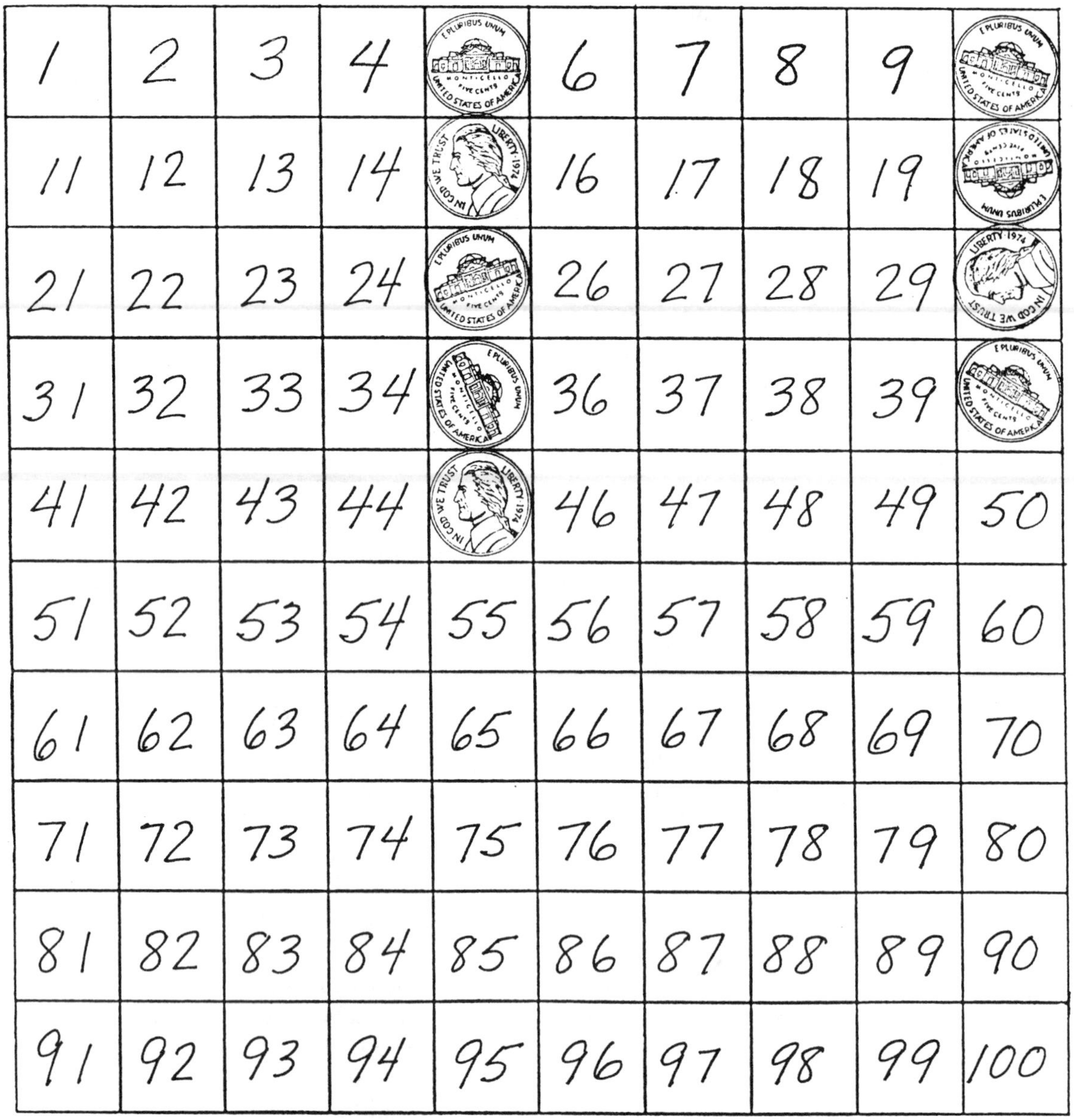

1	2	3	4		6	7	8	9	
11	12	13	14		16	17	18	19	
21	22	23	24		26	27	28	29	
31	32	33	34		36	37	38	39	
41	42	43	44		46	47	48	49	50
51	52	53	54	55	56	57	58	59	60
61	62	63	64	65	66	67	68	69	70
71	72	73	74	75	76	77	78	79	80
81	82	83	84	85	86	87	88	89	90
91	92	93	94	95	96	97	98	99	100

Figure 9–1.
A hundred square
with nickels.

IN SCHOOL: COUNTING UP

Use whatever method you prefer for helping children to count change. One way is to have them place coins on a hundred square, beginning with coins of a single kind. To find the value of a handful of nickels, for example, they can count ahead five numbers at a time, placing a nickel on every fifth square as shown in Figure 9–1. If they need to find the value of a collection of different coins, you can suggest that they begin with the largest. A quarter, two dimes, a nickel, and three

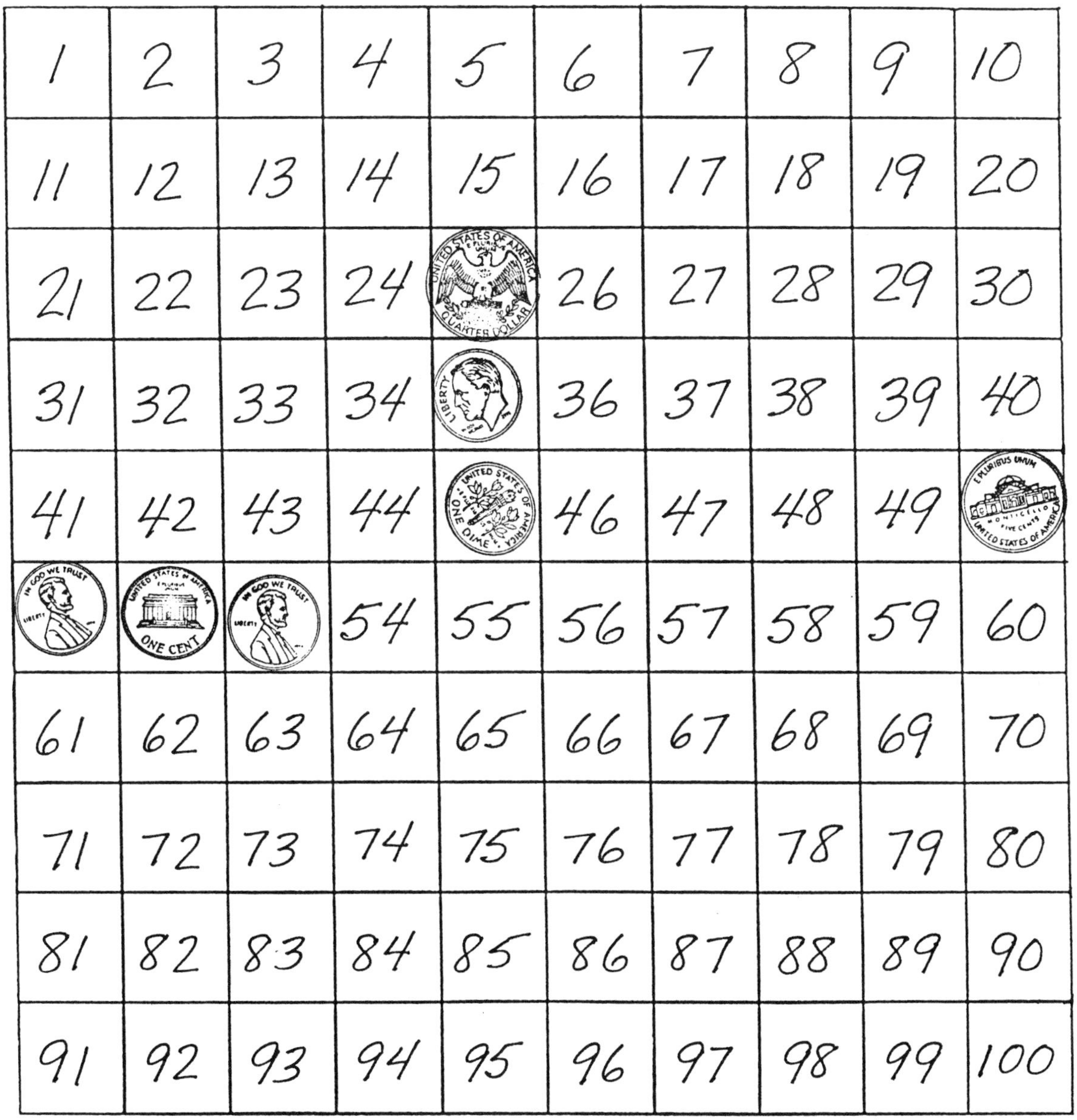

1	2	3	4	5	6	7	8	9	10
11	12	13	14	15	16	17	18	19	20
21	22	23	24	(quarter)	26	27	28	29	30
31	32	33	34	(dime)	36	37	38	39	40
41	42	43	44	(dime)	46	47	48	49	(nickel)
(penny)	(nickel)	(penny)	54	55	56	57	58	59	60
61	62	63	64	65	66	67	68	69	70
71	72	73	74	75	76	77	78	79	80
81	82	83	84	85	86	87	88	89	90
91	92	93	94	95	96	97	98	99	100

Figure 9–2.
A hundred square with fifty-three cents.

pennies would be placed on 25, 35 (ten ahead), 45, 50, 51, 52, and 53, showing 53¢ (see Figure 9–2). As they gain confidence, children will be able to do this without using the board.

AT HOME: COUNTING THE FAMILY'S CHANGE

Let parents know that children are learning to count change in school and suggest some practical situations in which they can hone their skills at home. Parents can put them in charge of counting out the exact change needed for the bus or laundromat or counting change received from the cashier in the supermarket. While waiting to make their own purchases children can see whether they have the coins needed to give the cashier exactly the right amount. Counting change just for fun is a good way to speed time while riding on a bus or waiting in the dentist's office.

BACK IN SCHOOL: MAKING PURCHASES

Hold a few coins in your hand, tell the children how much you're holding, and invite them to guess which coins you have. Write down the combinations they suggest. When there are no more suggestions, reveal the coins. The children can then play this game in pairs.

Your students can practice their change-counting skills in the classroom store. First ask them to price the items at any amounts less than a dollar. Help them make connections with the game they have played by holding up sample items with their price tags and asking for suggestions about which coins could be used to pay for them. Be sure there is enough play money in the purse so that customers can always pay with the exact change.

Making Change

Modern cash registers display the amount of change due the customer; the cashier doesn't need to compute it. In smaller stores, however, clerk and customer may not have this advantage. Making change is still a mental endeavor and a necessary skill.

In the classroom change is usually computed using formal subtraction, while at a store clerks draw change from the cash register, or verify it as they give it to the customer, by counting up from the price. Children may find it difficult to connect these two processes. A simple game, played in pairs, can encourage children to invent their own methods of computing change and also to count up. Later it will become the basis for relating these methods to subtraction.

IN SCHOOL: A CHANGE GAME

Give each pair of children a quarter's worth of change to start: a dime, two nickels, and five pennies. The change is placed on the table. While one player's eyes are closed the other takes a few coins. The player whose eyes were closed must guess the total amount of money the other is holding by looking at the coins that are left. The player who has taken the coins then shows them. Finally the money is returned to the table, smallest coins first, while the two players count up, starting with the money on the table, to check that they have the same amount they began with. The players then reverse roles. As children become skillful with this game you can increase the amount of change to 50¢, 75¢, or $1.

When children have had a chance to play this game for a while, ask them what strategies they used in making guesses. Some children may simply have tried to visualize the initial collection of coins to see which ones are missing. Others may have subtracted. Illustrate how both guessing and checking the result could be recorded:

Here's how you guessed
There was 25¢ on the table to begin with   25
You saw only 14¢   −14
The other 11¢ must have been taken   11

Here's how you checked
14¢ was on the table   14
11¢ more was returned to the table   +11
Then you had the 25¢ you started with   25

The next time they play the game ask the children to record each round.

AT HOME: TAKING CHARGE OF CHANGE

Ask children to play the game with someone at home. Also suggest to parents that they allow the child to hand money to the clerk when shopping and let them receive and count the change. Later they can examine the register receipt together to make sure the amount of change was correct. If the price (including tax) is known ahead of time, the child can choose what to give the cashier and predict the change that will be returned. You can also mention opportunities like bake sales, car washes, and yard sales, where children can serve alongside parents, making change for purchases.

BACK IN SCHOOL: PLAYING CASHIER

The role of the cashier in your classroom store can now be expanded to making change. This will be necessary if the customer is given only quarters and bills, while the cashier has a supply of smaller change. Customers should, of course, always count their change.

If you wish, you can run a training session for cashiers, letting them verify that they understand how to make change by completing a worksheet like the one in Figure 9–3. Successful completion earns

Cashier trainee's name *Grace*

$1.37

85¢   59¢   51¢

What coins would you give each customer in change?

1) Rada wants the baseball cards. She gives you a dollar.

15¢

2) Nathan gives you a dollar and two quarters for the book.

13¢

3) Liu hands you three quarters. He wants the frisbee.

16¢

4) Karen would like to buy the doll sweater. She gives you two quarters and a dime.

9¢

Figure 9–3.
Cashier trainee
worksheet.
(A reproducible
master for this from
is included in the
Appendix.)

the qualified cashier a certificate, to be posted in the store when the cashier is serving.

Saving for Purchases

Good money management requires more than being able to count money and make change. On a recent TV program, a group of upper elementary school children were asked where they thought money came from. Most said that money came from banks. A smaller group thought it came from their parents. Quite a few children said they did not know, and only a small percentage connected money with working. Clearly, we need to acquaint children with the means by which money is acquired. Planning and budgeting also involve being able to predict what one's expenses will be.

IN SCHOOL: CATALOG SHOPPING

Collect catalogs or newspaper advertising supplements—enough so that there is at least one for each pair of children. Duplicate an order form, with columns for listing items, quantities, and prices. Allot a certain amount of "spending money" to each pair and ask them to choose the items they would buy if that were all they had to spend. Calculators will be helpful in checking out various combinations of items, but also encourage mental estimation. Have each pair fill out an order form when they have made their selections. Older students can include tax and shipping charges.

When all the groups have finished, ask what kinds of decisions they had to make. Did they have to choose between a high-priced item and a number of lower-priced selections, for example? Did they have to give up some desired things in order to buy others?

Afterward you can brainstorm some ideas about where the money for these purchases might come from: saving from allowances? birthday gifts? the tooth fairy? earnings? How do the children in your class earn money? Do they have any other ideas about how money can be earned?

AT HOME: PLANNING A PURCHASE

Ask each child to plan a savings program to buy something he or she wants. Since family financial circumstances vary greatly, care must be taken to respect these. You could consider sending home a letter similar to the one in Figure 9–4.

BACK IN SCHOOL: A CLASS PURCHASE

With your class, make plans to purchase something the children really want for the classroom—a rabbit, for example. First they will have to determine how much it will cost; then they have to decide how to earn the money. It is relatively easy to find the price of a rabbit by calling or visiting a pet store, but what will the rabbit live in? How much do cages cost? What will it eat? Will you have to buy the food or can food be donated by families or gotten from waste thrown out by supermarket produce departments? Discuss these sorts of things so that the children can do the research necessary and make a list of all the costs involved.

Where will the money come from? Ask the children how they earned money for their personal purchases and make a list. This may suggest some things the class as a whole could do. Brainstorm other

Dear Parents,

In class, we've been working on planning for saving and spending. To enable the children to understand this personally I would like to ask each one, with your help, to plan a savings program for buying something he or she wants or a gift for someone else. Here are some of the things you can do:

1. Talk about whether the item your child has chosen is realistic, and if not, help choose another.

2. Help find out how much it would cost.

3. Ask how much your child already has to spend and help figure out how much more must be saved.

4. Think together about where the money will come from (allowances, earnings, etc.) and how much time it will take to save the amount needed.

5. Have your child make a plan for saving and help him or her follow the plan.

6. Make the final purchase a special occasion.

I hope this project will give you and your child lots of opportunity to talk about managing money. Happy planning!

Sincerely,

Figure 9–4.
Letter to parents about learning to save money. (A reproducible master for this form letter is included in the Appendix.)

fund-raising ideas. From your list have the children choose two or three to carry out. From here on, the specifics of planning will depend on the fund-raising methods chosen. You could consider having the class open a bank account as described in the next section. The more you can involve students in both planning and implementation, the more experience they will gain in making money management decisions.

Managing a Bank Account

Aside from formal instruction in how to write a check, dealing with bank accounts is something many people do not encounter until they first venture out into the world of work. In fact, balancing a checkbook seems to be the one most cumbersome task mentioned when adults are asked about how they use mathematics. Keeping personal accounts might be less onerous if it were introduced earlier.

IN SCHOOL:
REAL BANKS AND IMAGINARY ACCOUNTS

Ask the students what they know about banks and what they would like to find out. Then plan a trip to a local bank. Before the trip let the bank employee who will be leading the tour know what your class is most interested in seeing. In addition to things the students have said they would like to see, you could ask for an explanation of what happens to money between the time it is deposited and the time it is withdrawn. How does the bank earn money? What services does it provide in addition to savings and checking accounts? What is the difference between a savings account and a checking account?

Also ask the bank for a set of sample checks, deposit slips, and a record book, all of which you can photocopy when you return to school so that the students can set up imaginary accounts in the classroom. Each student can have an imaginary personal account or can open an imaginary joint account with another student. Every day "give" the class an amount to deposit. Each student or pair should fill out a deposit slip, enter the deposit on the record sheet, and figure out the balance. Then they can write one check for an item they want to buy (but not for more than is in the account), enter the check, and again compute the balance. The deposit slip and check should go to you.

At the end of the week give every accountholder a list of the deposits and checks you have received, and your statement of the balance in the account. Ask them to mark deposits and checks on the record sheet if they are correctly recorded. The balance on their sheet should match yours. If not, one of you has made an error, which must be found.

AT HOME: SAVINGS ACCOUNTS

Let parents know about your classroom account and suggest that if they are thinking of opening a savings account for their child, this might be a good time to do it. As an alternative, parents and children can set up a home bank. Parents act as bankers for their children, putting money in safekeeping when children "deposit" it using an appropriate deposit slip, and giving it back when a withdrawal slip is presented. Send home some photocopied withdrawal and deposit slips to parents who want to try this. Some parents may even be willing to let their children write out the checks (except for the signature) when they are paying bills.

BACK IN SCHOOL: OPENING A REAL ACCOUNT

The experiences students have had at school and at home will be good preparation for maintaining a real bank account. Think about opening a class account in which funds for special projects are deposited. Students should be in charge of making deposits and withdrawals and keeping records for this account (though you may need to be the courier and cosigner of checks). The responsibility can be rotated weekly among teams of three or four, with reports made to the class at the end of each tour of duty.

Becoming a Price-Conscious Consumer

Price-consciousness isn't all there is to being a thoughtful consumer, but it is certainly an important aspect of family economics. Adults who watch their pocketbooks do comparison shopping, save coupons, take advantage of sales and specials, and patronize discount stores and yard sales. Children can learn a great deal by participating in such activities and making decisions about which products to buy or where to shop.

A HOME/SCHOOL PROJECT: DOES THAT COUPON REALLY SAVE MONEY?

Appeal to parents for coupons they don't want to use. Have the students look for the expiration date on the coupons and discard any that are outdated. Then ask them to sort the coupons into different categories: cereal, soap, canned goods, etc. Which type of product seems to rely most heavily on coupons to attract shoppers? Coupons in each category can be arranged in order of expiration date to make it easy to keep the collection current.

Ask each student to select a coupon for a product he or she particularly likes. If there is a supermarket within walking distance, take a trip there to let students look for the products for which they have coupons. (Call the manager first to explain what you will be doing and make sure it will not interfere with business.) Give each student a sheet (see Figure 9–5) on which to record (1) whether the product is on the shelf, (2) what sizes are available and the weight or volume of each size, (3) competing brands and the price of each size for each brand, and (4) whether there are any special offers, such as double coupons. If it is not possible to visit a supermarket as a class, students can gather this information the next time they go to a grocery store with their parents.

Back in the classroom have the students compare the costs. Would using the coupon have saved money? How much? If not, which other brand would be the best buy? Was it the store's own brand? Does it always save money to use coupons?

Older students can also compute the unit prices of the products they found (see "Computing Unit Prices: Division" in Chapter 6) and compare them. An interesting question to ponder when shopping with coupons is which size offers the best buy. Using a coupon to buy the smallest size often results in a larger drop in the unit price than using it to buy larger sizes. Comparing unit prices will reveal this. There are also other factors to be considered. How much of the product do you need? If you need more than the small size offers, would it make sense to buy two of the smallest packages, using a

COUPON SHOPPING

My coupon was for 50¢ for Maxwell House Coffe

It was good for the following sizes: All Sizes

I (did) (did not) find it on the shelf. the small size

COST COMPARISON

Figure 9–5.
Coupon shopping
chart. (A repro-
ducible master
for this form is
included in the
Appendix.)

BRAND	SIZE	WEIGHT OR VOLUME	COST
Maxwell House Columbian	Large	24oz	5.45
Yuban Columbian	"	26oz	7.39
MJB Columbian	"	24oz	3.99
Taster's Choice	"	24oz	2.59

coupon for one, or to use the coupon for a single large package? Decisions like these are not easily made on the spot in the supermarket, but analyzing a few examples will help students become aware of such considerations.

Understanding Interest

Few people squirrel away large amounts of money at home. Banks are not only for safekeeping; they also provide a way to make money grow, to keep up with inflation. Children need to become aware of both of these functions.

IN SCHOOL: THE MONEY POT

Show the class your "money pot." When you put money in the pot, it grows. Here's how it happens: Each night the Interest Imp, who lives in the pot, counts the money and adds one dollar for every ten dollars she finds in the pot. (Since she doesn't have any change, she doesn't bother with amounts less than ten dollars.)

On Monday, put one hundred play dollars in the pot and seal it. Ask the students to predict how much money will be in the pot on Friday morning. Give them some time to think about and discuss this in small groups. Record the predictions.

Open the pot on Friday and count the contents (which you have increased to $146). Were any of the predictions correct? If so, ask the successful groups to show how they arrived at their predictions. Hand out the worksheet shown in Figure 9–6 for them to use to calculate the increase, and get students started by doing the first step. If no group was successful, start with $100; if correct predictions were made, begin with another sum.

Tell the students that banks are like the money pot, except that money in a bank does not grow so quickly. Show a bank advertisement which gives the interest rate. If the rate is 5 percent explain that this means the bank would add five dollars every year for every one hundred dollars in an account, although some banks divide this up and add the money every month or even every day.

AT HOME: FAMILY BANK INTEREST RATES

Ask the children to talk with their parents about banks. What kinds of accounts does their bank offer and what are the rates of interest for each account? Why do parents put money in a checking account if a savings or money market account gives more interest? Parents may be willing to show them the lines on bank statements in which interest has been added to their accounts, or to work out how much their children could earn by depositing whatever they have saved in a savings account at the family bank.

BACK IN SCHOOL: COMPUTING INTEREST

Give the children calculators and show them how to compute the amount of *principal* plus *interest* for an account that has been open for a year and is earning interest at a specified rate, say 5 percent. On most calculators, they simply have to enter the principal and press +, the interest rate (5), and %. The calculator will show the total. Pressing these keys three times in succession will show the amount to which an account has grown after three years.

Older students can deal with interest rates that involve fractions. Students can convert 5¼ percent to 5.25 percent before following the above procedure. You can also discuss the fact that if the bank adds interest more frequently than once a year (*compounds* the interest),

THE MONEY POT

DAY OF THE WEEK	AMOUNT IN THE POT	NUMBER OF TENS	AMOUNT ADDED
Monday	$100	10	$10
Tuesday	$110	11	$11
Wednesday	$121	12	$12
Thursday	$131	13	$13
Friday	$146	--------	-------

Figure 9–6. "The money pot" worksheet. (A reproducible master for this form is included in the Appendix.)

the actual interest will be more than the rate given. The actual rate is called the *yield*. By looking at bank advertisements they will be able to see the differences between the annual interest rate and the yield. If your class has studied percentages, you may want to have them do their own computations and compare the results with those given on the calculator.

Becoming a well-informed money manager takes years of experience. Children can learn a great deal from the practical wisdom gained by the adults in their families who have this experience. Relating family practice to what they are learning in school will help to put this knowledge at their fingertips when it is needed.

Chapter 10   Telephone Math

10
Telephone Math

The telephone has become an indispensable part of our lives. Yet in spite of our dependence on it, most of us take little conscious notice of the numerical system that allows us to reach friends and family in just a few seconds. Try to sketch from memory the dial or keypad you use every day to make calls. If you're like most other people, you won't be able to reproduce it accurately. In this respect we know little more than young children just learning to use the phone.

Since many of the activities in this chapter deal with the mathematics that can be found in phone numbers and phone books, parents and children will be able to work together as almost equal partners.

Learning About Phone Numbers

SCHOOL PROJECT: READING, WRITING, AND DIALING PHONE NUMBERS

Most kindergarten rooms have a house corner equipped with kitchen stove, doll beds, child-sized furniture, and a play phone. Some teachers have real phones in the playhouse—discarded or donated rotary or push-button models. Two phones will be needed for good dramatic play.

Children love to dial or push the buttons of a real phone and then have "adult" telephone conversations. To build on this interest, you can encourage them to learn to read and dial their home phone numbers. In large letters, write children's names and phone numbers on strips of tagboard, put the strips in a box near the house corner, and encourage the children to find and use their own numbers and those of their friends when making phone calls on the play phones.

When children have memorized their phone numbers and can dial them without error, send home a brief note informing parents of this accomplishment. Encourage the parents to let their children call home whenever such a call needs to be made.

In first- and second-grade classrooms, all you will need for a small phone area is a table with two phones, children's phone numbers filed alphabetically in a box, and pencil and paper for children to practice writing phone numbers. The phone area will soon become a popular choice during activity time. Here too, you can tell parents when their children have learned to read and dial their phone numbers.

With your help, first and second graders can make their own phone books in which they list the numbers of their friends and relatives. This "grown-up" activity—almost always popular with children of this age—provides additional practice in reading and writing numbers. Older children also enjoy making personal phone books.

Phone Number Patterns

Something as commonplace as telephone numbers can lead to interesting mathematical discoveries. The following activities involve children in examining their own and other phone numbers in an attempt to detect patterns. Begin by asking the children to write their names and telephone numbers in large print on strips of cardboard.

IN SCHOOL: ANALYZING PHONE NUMBERS

Tell the children to circulate around the room holding their cards and, without speaking, to join one other person whose number is like theirs in some way. When everyone is paired, the children can report to the class how their numbers are alike.

Did any two numbers begin with the same three digits? Perhaps all of them have this in common? If not, ask the children to move about again quietly and get together with all the people they can find whose numbers begin with the same three digits as theirs.

Talk about the fact that these first three numbers tell you to which *telephone exchange* you belong. Most phone books have a list of the exchanges in the local calling area. Some phone companies call these first three numbers the "prefix." You may find a "prefix location guide" in your phone book, or a map showing the location of the exchange or prefix numbers. In small communities or rural areas, there may be only one exchange. In larger cities, there will be many different ones.

Ask the children whose phone numbers have the same prefix to share their addresses. Did they find out that they lived in the same part of town? If your phone book has a prefix map, enlarge it and have the children put their names in the appropriate places. If no prefix map is available, an outline city map can be used instead.

After the students have studied their phone number prefixes, post all the strips showing their names and phone numbers on the bulletin board. Children with the same prefix will immediately see that the remaining four digits of their phone numbers are all different. Every four-digit grouping is unique.

When the students look at the list of complete phone numbers, ask them whether they see any patterns or other interesting things. Tell them that we call the individual numbers *digits*. List the things they notice, which may include:

- Numbers with repeated digits.
- Numbers whose digits are all odd or all even.
- Numbers whose digits alternate: odd, even, odd, even.
- Numbers that include consecutive digits (234, 5678, 987, etc.).
- Numbers that start and end with the same digit.
- Palindromes (numbers that read the same forward and backward).

If they are slow getting started, ask them specifically if they see any numbers with one of these characteristics—palindromes, digits that repeat, consecutive digits, etc.

AT HOME: A PATTERN SEARCH

Most families have a personal telephone directory, an address book, or a list of frequently called numbers posted on the wall or the refrigerator. As a family assignment, give each child a copy of the worksheet in Figure 10–1, to be used with their personal phone list. While they are looking for phone number patterns, children can ask family members how they memorize phone numbers. Do they use pattern tricks for remembering special numbers?

Some phone companies will give you a choice of easy-to-remember numbers when you get a phone. (This may involve an extra charge.) If your company is one of these, students and their families may be interested in knowing about it.

BACK IN SCHOOL: SHARING PATTERNS

Make a chart showing all the types of patterns families found in their phone lists, with examples of each. Ask the students to report if their families used any tricks to remember telephone numbers. Then have them create their own list of easy-to-remember numbers and explain why they think they are easy.

PATTERNS

IN THE ___Larson's___ FAMILY'S PHONE LIST

These numbers have repeated digits:

443-7229 _____ 449-2160 _____

These numbers have all even digits:

666-2042 _____ 442-6284 _____

These numbers have all odd digits:

none _____ _____ _____

These numbers have some digits which go up or down in order.

321-8513 _____ 791-2468 _____

Here are some other patterns we found:

Figure 10–1.
Phone number pattern worksheet.
(A reproducible master for this form is included in the Appendix.)

PATTERN	NUMBER
Palindrome	440-3883
Every other number is even	254-2761
There are no #s above 3	222-2013

Area Code Patterns

Why study area codes? A close examination of these codes will reveal a variety of patterns that in turn raise some interesting questions. Is there a system to the assignment of codes? Patterns lead to questions in mathematics, too. Searching for patterns in real-life situations and thinking about their significance is good preparation for doing the same sort of thinking in mathematics.

To get a sense of some of the questions that can be raised by the patterns (or lack of patterns) in area codes, spend some time yourself studying the area code pages in your phone book. Your own interest and enthusiasm will help to stimulate your students' thinking.

At the beginning of most telephone books, there are one or two pages devoted to area codes. Almost all phone books have a chart (see Figure 10–2 for an example) that lists area codes by state—from Alabama to the Virgin Islands. Some phone books also include a table listing area codes in numerical order—from 201 (New Jersey) to 919 (North Carolina)—see Figure 10–3, and many show the geographic distribution of area codes and time zones on a U.S. map (see Figure 10–4).

IN SCHOOL: BECOMING AWARE OF AREA CODES

Find out whether your students already know about area codes by asking what number you should dial if you wanted to call one of them from a distant city. You can explain the need for an area code if no one brings it up. What is your area code? Do the children know the area codes for any of the places their families call frequently? If not, you could send one or two students to the school office to ask whether the office staff makes long distance calls and to which area codes.

Write all the area codes you have gathered on the board, including patterns the children see or observations they have made.

AT HOME: LOOKING FOR PATTERNS IN AREA CODES

Give all the students a copy of the Figure 10–2 and ask them to study the chart with their parents to see if additional patterns can be found. Students can also look for places where relatives or friends live and take note of their area codes. Since phone books in different parts of the country do not list all the same cities, encourage the students to compare the chart handed out (which is from a Colorado phone book) with the chart published in their state. What differences can they find? Is there an explanation for the differences? Patterns, questions, and observations should be written down and brought to school.

BACK IN SCHOOL: QUESTIONS ABOUT AREA CODES

Distribute photocopies of Figures 10–2, 10–3, and 10–4 to pairs or small groups of students. Ask them to study the charts carefully and

LONG DISTANCE Area Codes

LOCATION	AREA CODE
Alabama (AL)	
all locations	205
Alaska (AK)	
all locations	907
Arizona (AZ)	
all locations	602
Arkansas (AR)	
all locations	501
California (CA)	
Anaheim	714
Bakersfield	805
Barstow	619
Eureka	707
Fresno	209
Long Beach	310
Los Angeles	213
Modesto	209
Monterey	408
Oakland	510
Palm Springs	619
Pasadena	818
Riverside	909
Sacramento	916
San Bernardino	909
San Diego	619
San Francisco	415
San Jose	408
Santa Barbara	805
Colorado (CO)	
Aspen	303
Boulder	303
Colorado Springs	719
Denver	303
Durango	303
Grand Junction	303
Leadville	719
Pueblo	719
Steamboat Springs	303
Connecticut (CT)	
all locations	203
Delaware (DE)	
all locations	302
District of Columbia (DC)	
Washington	202
Florida (FL)	
Ft. Lauderdale	305
Ft. Myers	813
Jacksonville	904
Key West	305
Miami	305
Orlando	407
Pensacola	904
St. Petersburg	813
Tallahassee	904
Tampa	813
West Palm Beach	407
Georgia (GA)	
Albany	912
Atlanta Metro	404
Augusta	706
Columbus	706
Rome	706
Savannah	912
Hawaii (HI)	
all locations	808
Idaho (ID)	
all locations	208

LOCATION	AREA CODE
Illinois (IL)	
Alton	618
Cairo	618
Champaign-Urbana	217
Chicago	312
Chicago Suburbs	708
Elgin	708
La Salle	815
Mt. Vernon	618
Peoria	309
Rockford	815
Rock Island	309
Springfield	217
Waukegan	708
Indiana (IN)	
Evansville	812
Gary	219
Hammond	219
Indianapolis	317
Kokomo	317
Michigan City	219
South Bend	219
Iowa (IA)	
Council Bluffs	712
Davenport	319
Des Moines	515
Dubuque	319
Sioux City	712
Kansas (KS)	
Dodge City	316
Lawrence	913
Salina	913
Topeka	913
Wichita	316
Kentucky (KY)	
Ashland	606
Frankfort	502
Louisville	502
Paducah	502
Shelbyville	502
Winchester	606
Louisiana (LA)	
Baton Rouge	504
Lake Charles	318
New Orleans	504
Shreveport	318
Maine (ME)	
all locations	207
Maryland (MD)	
Annapolis	410
Baltimore	410
Hagerstown	301
Rockville	301
Massachusetts (MA)	
Boston	617
Fall River	508
New Bedford	508
Pittsfield	413
Springfield	413
Worcester	508
Michigan (MI)	
Ann Arbor	313
Bay City	517
Battle Creek	616
Detroit	313
Flint	313
Grand Rapids	616
Jackson	517
Kalamazoo	616
Lansing	517
Marquette	906
Sault Ste. Marie	906

LOCATION	AREA CODE
Minnesota (MN)	
Duluth	218
Minneapolis	612
Rochester	507
St. Paul	612
Mississippi (MS)	
all locations	601
Missouri (MO)	
Columbia	314
Jefferson City	314
Joplin	417
Kansas City	816
St. Joseph	816
St. Louis	314
Springfield	417
Montana (MT)	
all locations	406
Nebraska (NE)	
Lincoln	402
North Platte	308
Omaha	402
Scottsbluff	308
Nevada (NV)	
all locations	702
New Hampshire (NH)	
all locations	603
New Jersey (NJ)	
Atlantic City	609
Camden	609
Hackensack	201
Jersey City	201
Newark	201
New Brunswick	908
Paterson	201
Trenton	609
Vineland	609
New Mexico (NM)	
all locations	505
New York (NY)	
Albany	518
Binghamton	607
Bronx	718 (cellular 917)
Brooklyn	718 (cellular 917)
Buffalo	716
Elmira	607
Hempstead	516
Long Island	516
Manhattan	212 (cellular 917)
Niagara Falls	716
Peekskill	914
Poughkeepsie	914
Queens	718 (cellular 917)
Rochester	716
Schenectady	518
Staten Island	718 (cellular 917)
Syracuse	315
Troy	518
Utica	315
White Plains	914
Yonkers	914
North Carolina (NC)	
Asheville	704
Charlotte	704
Fayetteville	919
Greensboro	919
Raleigh	919
Winston-Salem	919
North Dakota (ND)	
all locations	701

LOCATION	AREA CODE
Ohio (OH)	
Akron	216
Canton	216
Cincinnati	513
Cleveland	216
Columbus	614
Dayton	513
Lorain	216
Steubenville	614
Toledo	419
Youngstown	216
Oklahoma (OK)	
Enid	405
Oklahoma City	405
Tulsa	918
Oregon (OR)	
all locations	503
Pennsylvania (PA)	
Allentown	215
Altoona	814
Erie	814
Harrisburg	717
Philadelphia	215
Pittsburgh	412
Reading	215
Scranton	717
Wilkes-Barre	717
Rhode Island (RI)	
all locations	401
South Carolina (SC)	
all locations	803
South Dakota (SD)	
all locations	605
Tennessee (TN)	
Chattanooga	615
Knoxville	615
Memphis	901
Nashville	615
Texas (TX)	
Abilene	915
Amarillo	806
Austin	512
Beaumont	409
Brownsville	512
Corpus Christi	512
Dallas	214
El Paso	915
Fort Worth	817
Galveston	409
Houston	713
Laredo	210
Lubbock	806
San Antonio	210
Tyler	903
Waco	817
Utah (UT)	
all locations	801
Vermont (VT)	
all locations	802
Virginia (VA)	
Alexandria	703
Arlington	703
Charlottesville	804
Newport News	804
Norfolk	804
Richmond	804
Roanoke	703

LOCATION	AREA CODE
Washington (WA)	
Seattle	206
Spokane	509
Tacoma	206
Vancouver	206
Walla Walla	509
Yakima	509
Washington DC (District of Columbia)	
all locations	202
West Virginia (WV)	
all locations	304
Wisconsin (WI)	
Eau Claire	715
Fond du Lac	414
Green Bay	414
Madison	608
Milwaukee	414
Racine	414
Wausau	715
Wyoming (WY)	
all locations	307
CANADA	
Alberta (AB)	
all locations	403
British Columbia (BC)	
all locations	604
Manitoba (MB)	
all locations	204
New Brunswick (NB)	
all locations	506
Newfoundland (NF)	
all locations	709
Nova Scotia (NS)	
all locations	902
Ontario (ON)	
*Hamilton	905
London	519
*Mississauga	905
*Niagra Falls	905
North Bay	705
Ottawa	613
Sault Ste. Marie	705
Thunder Bay	807
Toronto (Metro)	416
Prince Edward Island (PE)	
all locations	902
Quebec (PQ)	
Montreal	514
Quebec City	418
Saskatchewan (SK)	
all locations	306
Mexico (MX)	
See International Calls page.	
Puerto Rico (PR)	
all locations	809
Virgin Islands (VI)	
all locations	809

*Effective as of October 2, 1993

Dial "O" (operator) if the area code you need is not listed above or cannot be found on the Time Zones Map.

Figure 10–2. (*opposite*) Long distance area codes.

write down any questions they may have as well as patterns they found. Students of two fourth-grade classes, working in groups of four and five, came up with the following questions, which we've organized under appropriate headings.

How are area codes made up and assigned?

- How did they decide which states got which area codes? Why didn't they use letters?
- Who makes up the codes? Is it a person or a computer?
- What do they do when they run out of area codes?

Area codes in different states and countries

- Why does each city or town have a code?
- Why are there the same area codes in one state?
- Why do states have more than one area code?
- Does the population affect the area code?
- Why does New York have so many codes?
- How many area codes are there in the US?
- Why are Mexico and Canada included in the US area code system?
- How come Canada has very few area codes?
- Do different countries have more or less digits in their area codes?
- Are there area codes around the world?
- Why do places have area codes?

Figure 10–3. Long distance area codes in numerical order.

States or provinces that are served by more than one area code are shown by an asterisk (*).

AREA CODES
In numerical order, to help you identify your calls.

**Effective as of November 1, 1992
***Effective as of November 14, 1992
†Effective as of October 2, 1993

Area Code	Location	Area Code	Location	Area Code	Location	Area Code	Location	Area Code	Location	Area Code	Location
* 201	New Jersey	307	Wyoming	* 413	Massachusetts	* 519	Ontario	* 707	California	* 815	Illinois
202	Dist. of Columbia	* 308	Nebraska	* 414	Wisconsin	601	Mississippi	* 708	Illinois	* 816	Missouri
203	Connecticut	* 309	Illinois	* 415	California	602	Arizona	709	Newfoundland	* 817	Texas
204	Manitoba	* 310	California	* 416	Ontario	603	New Hampshire		and Labrador	818	California
205	Alabama	* 312	Illinois	* 417	Missouri	604	Brit. Columbia	* 712	Iowa	* 819	Quebec
* 206	Washington	* 313	Michigan	* 418	Quebec	605	South Dakota	* 713	Texas	* 901	Tennessee
207	Maine	* 314	Missouri	* 419	Ohio	* 606	Kentucky	* 714	California	902	P.E.I. and
208	Idaho	* 315	New York	501	Arkansas	* 607	New York	* 715	Wisconsin		Nova Scotia
* 209	California	* 316	Kansas	* 502	Kentucky	* 608	Wisconsin	* 716	New York	* 903	Texas
** 210	Texas	* 317	Indiana	503	Oregon	* 609	New Jersey	* 717	Pennsylvania	* 904	Florida
* 212	New York	* 318	Louisiana	* 504	Louisiana	* 612	Minnesota	* 718	New York	† 905	Ontario
* 213	California	* 319	Iowa	505	New Mexico	* 613	Ontario	* 719	Colorado	* 906	Michigan
* 214	Texas	401	Rhode Island	506	New Brunswick	* 614	Ohio	801	Utah	907	Alaska
* 215	Pennsylvania	* 402	Nebraska	* 507	Minnesota	* 615	Tennessee	802	Vermont	* 908	New Jersey
* 216	Ohio	403	Alberta, Yukon	* 508	Massachusetts	* 616	Michigan	803	South Carolina	***909	California
* 217	Illinois		and N.W. Terr.	* 509	Washington	* 617	Massachusetts	* 804	Virginia	* 912	Georgia
* 218	Minnesota	* 404	Georgia	* 510	California	* 618	Illinois	* 805	California	* 913	Kansas
* 219	Indiana	* 405	Oklahoma	* 512	Texas	* 619	California	* 806	Texas	* 914	New York
301	Maryland	406	Montana	* 513	Ohio	701	North Dakota	* 807	Ontario	* 915	Texas
302	Delaware	* 407	Florida	* 514	Quebec	702	Nevada	808	Hawaii	* 916	California
* 303	Colorado	* 408	California	* 515	Iowa	* 703	Virginia	809	Puerto Rico	* 917	New York
304	West Virginia	* 409	Texas	* 516	New York	* 704	North Carolina	* 812	Indiana	* 918	Oklahoma
* 305	Florida	* 410	Maryland	* 517	Michigan	* 705	Ontario	* 813	Florida	* 919	North Carolina
306	Saskatchewan	* 412	Pennsylvania	* 518	New York	* 706	Georgia	* 814	Pennsylvania		

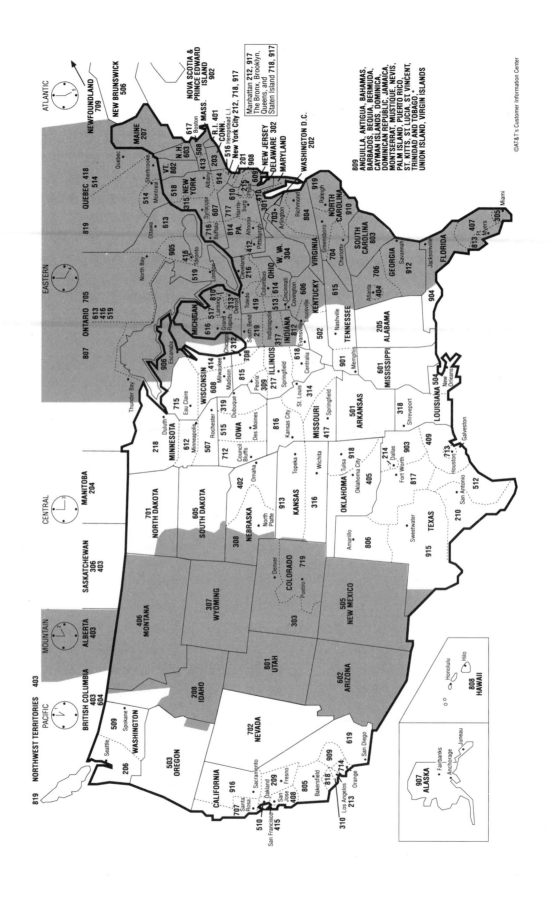

©AT&T's Customer Information Center

Figure 10–4.
(*opposite*) A
time zones/area
codes map.

Do the actual numbers of the codes have any significance?

- Why do the lower-population states have one area code but the number of the code is high?
- Do the higher-number area codes have to do with more population?
- Why do many southern states have high area codes?
- Why does New Jersey have the lowest area code?

Order of area codes

- Why aren't the area codes in order by state?
- Why do area codes bounce around?
- Why isn't Delaware 001 then the state assigned next would be 002?
- Why does Colorado have 303 and 719 for codes? Why not 303 and 304?
- Why are area codes beginning with 8 spread out through the country?

Patterns in area codes

- Why are there three numbers in an area code?
- Why aren't there any area codes starting with 1?
- Why do they start at 2 and skip 1?
- Why is there only 0 or 1 in the middle?
- Why aren't there any 11's in area codes?

If the students have a chance to discuss their questions, they may be able to find plausible answers for some of them. The telephone company may also be able to answer questions. Have the students mail their questions to the phone company so that they can be referred to a knowledgeable person.

The "What do they do when they run out of area codes?" question is very timely. Under the current numbering system, the middle digit of an area code is *always* either a 0 or a 1, and the three-digit prefix *never* includes a 0 or a 1. This was done so area codes and prefixes wouldn't ever duplicate one another and computers could automatically tell which was which. Since all the possible area code combinations have been used up, it is now necessary to create area codes where the second digit is not a 1 or a 0. This means that subscribers will have to dial the area code even when making a long-distance call within the same calling area so that phone company computers will thus be able to recognize the first three numbers as an area code, not a prefix.

Figure 10–4.
(*opposite*) A
time zones/area
codes map.

ADDITIONAL FAMILY HOMEWORK

Ask students and parents to figure out how many area codes are possible if the middle digit must be 0 or 1.

ADDITIONAL AREA CODE RESEARCH

If students think that the number of area codes in a state is related to its size, displaying a large map of the United States will help to answer this question.

If the size of a state does not seem to determine the number of its area codes, what does determine it? Older students may relate the number of area codes in a state to population density. These students can do additional research to find out when the various area codes were assigned. The phone company should have this information for local area codes. With the help of the school librarian, students can also check population figures to find out how much a state's population had increased when a new area code was assigned.

Since several of the fourth graders doing area code research raised questions about the location of different codes, the phone book map with area codes could also be examined more closely.

Phone Book Estimation

Estimating is sometimes defined as educated guessing. We estimate when we need not an exact answer but a "ballpark" figure, an approximation of the exact answer. We also estimate when it is difficult or impossible to obtain an exact answer. Counting all the names in the telephone book would take an absurd amount of time, but an estimation can be obtained rather quickly.

Children who have been schooled in producing right answers may be uncomfortable with estimation at first. Asked to estimate a sum, for example, they sometimes actually add first and then round off the result. For such children, the phone book activities that follow are a good way of easing into estimation because exact counts are impossible to obtain in a short period of time.

IN SCHOOL: ESTIMATING LISTINGS

First, have the children guess how many listings there are in the white pages of your telephone book and record their guesses on the board. Do they have reasons for their guesses? Next, divide your class into small groups, give each group a phone book, and tell the students that you will give them plenty of time to make a more careful estimate. Some groups may decide to count the names in one column, then multiply this number by the number of columns per page and the number of pages in the phone book. Other groups may take different approaches. Regardless of the methods used, students should be able to explain why they think their estimates are reasonable. See what estimates the children come up with, let them compare their estimates, and then let each group describe how they arrived at their final figure.

Phone Book Classification

Some parents may wonder why classification appears as a mathematical topic. Remind them that classifying, or creating categories, requires logical thinking—a very important aspect of mathematics. (See the discussion on classifying and sorting in Chapter 2.)

AT HOME AND IN SCHOOL: CLASSIFYING NAMES

Ask your students and their families to count the number of listings with their own last name and names of other branches of the family. Are any of these people relatives? Perhaps parents can share some family history here. Do they know the origin of their names? Can they explain why there are or aren't many other people in the area who share their name?

Back in school the children can compare the results of the searches they made at home. Some may want to use the estimate that the class made of the total number of listings in the white pages to calculate the fraction or percentage of listings with their own name. Others may enjoy browsing through the names in the white pages to look for certain categories. For instance: names of occupations (weaver, barber), names of animals (bear, wolf), names of colors (brown, green), names related to the weather (storm, snow), or to nature (stone, moon), and so on. Encourage the children to come up with additional categories.

Yellow Page Statistics

The yellow pages of your phone book contain a great deal of information; this information can stimulate discussions with children about what's available in their community, what isn't, and why. Organizing and analyzing this information may lead to some interesting conclusions.

IN SCHOOL: WHAT'S IN THE YELLOW PAGES FOR ME?

What kinds of businesses do the students in your room like to patronize—toy stores? video stores? ice cream shops? pizza parlors? Make a list of these as they are suggested. Then let pairs of students choose one type of business and count the listings in the yellow pages under that category. Display the results on a graph. Which types of business have the most listings? Why? Would you expect as many toy stores as grocery stores?

Older students can compute the ratio of different kinds of businesses to households in your region or community. For the number of households they can use your estimate of the total number of telephone listings in your phone book. In one large city, the ratio of pizza parlors to households was approximately 1:2000. How does this compare with your city or region? How does the ratio of video stores to households compare with the ratio of pet stores to households?

AT HOME:
FINDING FAMILY NEEDS IN THE YELLOW PAGES

Ask each family to list at least five kinds of businesses or services they use other than those their children listed in school. Then they should:

- Mark the ones they patronize.
- Identify the business in each category that is closest to their home.
- Count and record the number of listings in each category.

This can be an occasion for parents to talk about why they chose the particular businesses or services they use, and whether they think there are enough such services. If students have worked out ratios of businesses to households in school, they can also do this at home for each business or service on their family's list.

BACK IN SCHOOL:
HOW IS YOUR COMMUNITY SERVED?

Extend your list of community businesses and services as children bring in results from home. Let the children examine their data to see which businesses or services seem to be most in demand. Using their data they can plan an imaginary town or city of smaller or larger size. If there is one pizza parlor for every two thousand households in your region, how may pizza parlors would they plan for in a town with eight thousand households? Who might use this information?

The study and analysis of telephone numbers leads to interesting pattern searches. Although looking for number patterns is different from using math in everyday activities, many children become fascinated with the "pure math" of these patterns. Children who are not as interested in playing around with numbers may find the estimation, classification, and statistical explorations more to their liking. Both kinds of activities have their own momentum and offer parents and children wonderful opportunities to share interests, raise questions, research answers, and enjoy each other's company as partners in learning.

Chapter 11   Taking Care of the Mail

11
Taking Care of the Mail

When we collect our mail, many of us look first for the "real mail"—letters and cards from friends and relatives. Then we open the bills and put them in a pile, look to see what sweepstake we have "won," and glance at advertising and appeals for contributions. This mail-opening ritual almost always involves some mathematics. You sort the mail, add up the bills, estimate the odds, and evaluate the bargains. Responding to the mail involves even more mathematics. Do I have enough money in my account to pay the bills and make some contributions as well? Does this letter weigh more than two ounces? Do I have the right assortment of leftover stamps to put together the amount needed for overseas airmail postage?

Children get mail too—birthday cards and notes from relatives. They may also enjoy sending letters to friends or mailing letters and packages for their parents. Taking care of the mail gives parents and children almost daily opportunities to communicate about mathematics.

The Numbers on an Envelope

Almost every envelope in our mail contains a lot of numerical information. Since we are mostly interested in the content of the envelope, we pay little attention to the numbers on its face. But think how much children could learn from studying these numbers: there may be street numbers, house numbers, apartment numbers, postal route and postal box numbers, zip codes, numbers on the stamps, as well as the postal date stamp showing when the letter was mailed.

IN SCHOOL:
READING AND INTERPRETING NUMBERS

Bring a collection of used envelopes to class, or ask parents to save envelopes of letters they receive and send some to school for your number study. In small groups, the children can compare their envelopes. How many different numbers do they see? What do these numbers tell us? Ask each group to list the numbers on their envelopes, and encourage the students to find some categories. For instance:

- Which numbers would answer a "how much" question?
- Which numbers refer to "where from" and "where to"?
- Are there numbers that answer "when" questions?

A subsequent discussion with the children may give you a good idea of their understanding of all these numbers.

AT HOME: LOOKING FOR MORE NUMBERS

Ask parents to help their children look for more numbers in the family mail. They may notice that some of the numbers on the envelopes sent to their homes are always the same, others vary. Which ones stay the same? Can they explain why?

BACK IN SCHOOL: COMPARING NUMBERS

When children return with their home surveys, they can compare their findings. Which numbers are the same on each piece of mail, and which are different? (This will be a good time to learn what a zip code is.) Are there numbers that are the same for everyone in class?

Children may also enjoy playing around with some of their envelope numbers. Which are the longest? Which are the shortest? Can they find patterns? What other interesting observations can they make? If the children have enjoyed their explorations, they could end this project by compiling a class book, "The Numbers on an Envelope."

How Long Does It Take for a Letter to Be Delivered?

What happens to a letter after it is dropped into the mailbox? Children will know that a mail carrier delivers letters and packages to their homes or to their postal box; they may also have seen mail carriers empty mail boxes full of letters; but have they ever wondered what happens in between? Keeping records of the time it takes between mailing and delivery may make children curious as to what really does happen to the mail after it is picked up. It will also teach them to keep records, organize the information, and represent it graphically.

IN SCHOOL: WRITING AND MAILING LETTERS

To help your students find out how long it takes for a local letter to be delivered, divide the class into pairs: arrange the pairs so that some partners will live close to each other while others will live farther apart. Each child will write and address a letter to his or her partner. (Younger children may need help with this.) When the letters have been written, take your class for a walk to the nearest mailbox so each one can drop his or her letter in the box. Show the children where the pickup times are listed on the mailbox so they will see more mail-related numbers!

AT HOME: KEEPING RECORDS

Help the children make a simple chart they can take home and use to keep the following records:

1. Date, place, and time letter was mailed.
2. Date and time letter was received at home.
3. Date, place, and time reply was mailed.
4. Date and time reply was received at home.

Be sure each child has his or her partner's address. Ask the children to write down the date when their partner's letter arrives at their home and to send a reply to their partner's home address the following day, recording where and at what time the letter was mailed. Send a note home to parents announcing and explaining this project. Ask parents to help their children, if necessary, to keep the proper records and address the reply envelope.

Parents should record the approximate time of home mail delivery and pickup, and remind their children to read the pickup time on mailboxes if they mail their letters there.

BACK IN SCHOOL: GRAPHING RESULTS

When all the return letters have been received, the class will be ready to organize the data. Children can start out with one graph, showing the numbers of letters that took one, two, and three (or more) days to arrive (see Figure 11–1). A second set of graphs might show how long it took the letters that were mailed from the mailbox near school to arrive at the children's homes and how long it took the letters that were mailed from the children's homes to arrive at their friends' homes. Do these graphs show any differences in the time it took letters to arrive? What might account for the differences?

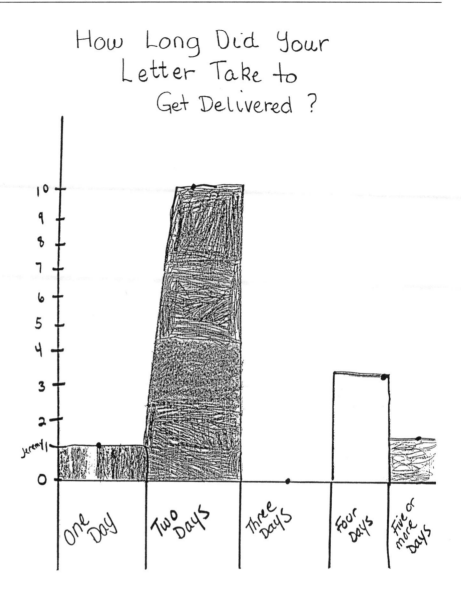

Figure 11–1.
Second graders chart the results of their mail survey.

Ask the children to write a story about what they think happens to a letter between the time it is mailed and the time it is received and have them read one another's stories. Make a list of the questions that come up in a discussion of the stories. Could the mail carrier who delivers the school mail spare a little time to talk to the class and answer some of these questions?

The story in Figure 11–2 shows that the children in a second-grade class have gained some understanding of where and when mail is picked up and delivered. A trip to the post office would be very beneficial in helping your students learn what happens between

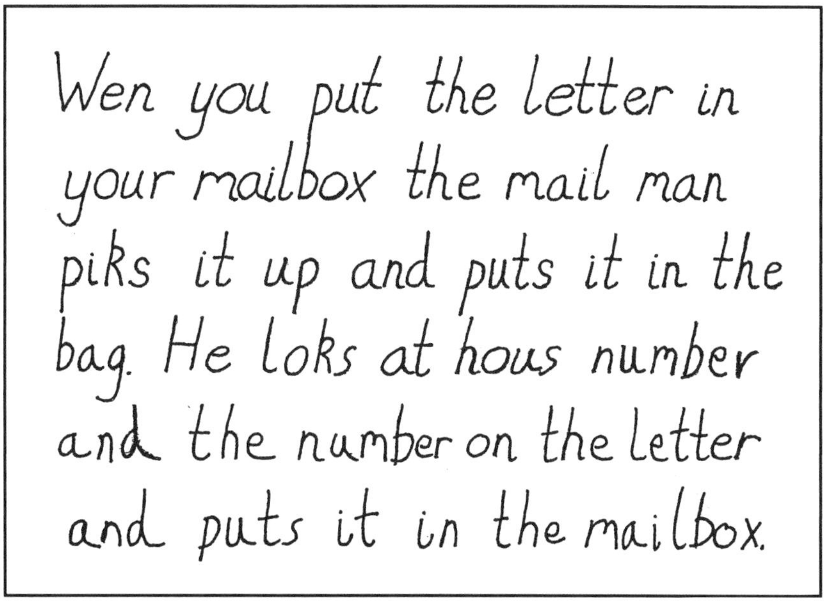

Figure 11–2.
A second grader
answers the ques-
tion, What happens
to your letter after
you drop it in the
mailbox?

> Wen you put the letter in your mailbox the mail man piks it up and puts it in the bag. He loks at hous number and the number on the letter and puts it in the mailbox.

pickup and delivery. It would be interesting to have the children write a similar story after the trip and compare it with their first story.

Behind the Scenes at the Post Office: Sorting, Weighing, and More

Organizing field trips takes a good deal of time, but what the children learn from such an excursion will make it well worth the extra effort.

Most children have been in a post office with their parents, or on their own, to buy stamps, pick up letters, or mail packages. Few of us, however, have had an opportunity to see the operations going on behind the counter where customers are served. Seeing and learning what happens "back there" puts children in touch with the workings of the real world, which almost always arouses their interest. After their letter-writing and -mailing project, a trip to the post office will enable the children to see the sequence in which incoming and outgoing mail is processed.

IN SCHOOL:
GETTING READY FOR THE POST OFFICE FIELD TRIP

Divide the class into groups of four or five and have the children brainstorm questions that they would like to get answered at the post office. Make a master list of the questions and organize it into categories like mail delivery, weighing mail, how mail travels, and so on. Give each child a copy of this new list to take along on the trip so they will remember their questions. See whether the children can decide who should ask the questions at the post office.

It would be very helpful if you can visit the post office yourself ahead of time and talk to the person who will be your guide. Let the guide know what you would like the children to see—postal scales of various sizes, sorting boxes and/or sorting machines, mailbags, local mail delivery vehicles and large mail trucks, mail carriers preparing their mail for delivery or bringing in mail for shipment, and so on. Tell the prospective guide what the children have done in school, and share the list of questions they have compiled. This will help him or her to plan for your visit.

IN SCHOOL: AFTER THE TRIP— PROCESSING NEW INFORMATION

Give the children a couple of days to think about the field trip—processing information takes time. Then ask the class how they want to present what they have learned. Here are some suggestions:

- Write a story describing what happens to a letter between mailing and delivery.
- Make a group mural, putting in everything you remember seeing.
- Make a sequence mural: get a roll of white wrapping paper, divide it into equal-sized segments, and then go over the various stages of mail processing that your students saw at the post office:

    What happens after the letter carrier empties the mailbox?

    What happens first at the post office when mail is brought in?

    What happens next? and next? and so on until the mail is in the letter carrier's bag or car, ready for delivery.

Each child illustrates a different stage of the process and writes a caption under his or her drawing.

A Classroom Post Office

Having been to a real post office and learned about its operation, both younger and older children can benefit from creating a post office in their classroom. Younger children learn about the jobs of the bigger world by role-playing what they have observed. Having a post office in their dramatic play area will enable the children to reenact—on their level of understanding—what they saw on their trip, and recreate the sequence of steps involved in processing mail. Older children don't want to "play post office"—they want the real thing. They will work hard at acquiring the necessary skills to perform the needed jobs: weighing in ounces, adding, subtracting, multiplying, and making change. With practice and some initial help, they are quite capable of running a small school post office.

SCHOOL PROJECT: HOW TO SET UP AND RUN A CLASSROOM POST OFFICE

Collect old envelopes, canceled stamps, and play money for younger children who want to write and mail letters and buy stamps at their post office. Try to supply the post office with date stamps and ink pads, a glue stick, and the various kinds of postal stickers you can get at the post office, as well as an old postal or other scale and a variety of sorting boxes. These items will enable the postal clerk to do his or her job. An old carryall will make a great letter bag for mail carriers to use to deliver their mail in the classroom (and perhaps, on prearranged occasions, in other rooms of the school).

Students from the third or fourth grade up can run a working post office for other school personnel—faculty, staff, and children—to visit at a certain time of day. If the office staff agrees, this working post office can take care of the school's outgoing mail as well as sell stamps to individuals. With the help of volunteers, children can also post letters at the nearest mailbox.

What skills would the children have to learn in order to become responsible postal clerks?

■ Since outgoing mail has to be weighed, children need to know how to use a scale. A postal scale would be nice to have but you can use a simple homemade one just as well (see "A Balance for Weighing Mail" in Figure 11–3). Students can make a chart showing the postage needed for various weights.

■ If they want to sell different combinations of stamps to make up the current first-class postage, they can make another chart showing various combinations of numbers adding up to this amount. Finding these combinations will give them good practice with addition.

■ Finally, children must know how to make change for their customers. Suggestions for learning this skill are given in Chapter 9.

A BALANCE FOR WEIGHING MAIL

Using a pair of pliers, squeeze the ends of a coat hanger together and bend up.

Punch four holes just below the rim of an 8-ounce yogurt cup. Cut three 16-inch pieces of string.

Thread the ends of two of the pieces of string through opposite holes in the cup and tie, leaving equal length loops.

Put the third string through the hole in the spring of a clothespin and tie the ends together.

Hang the cup and the clothespin on the bent-up ends of the hanger.

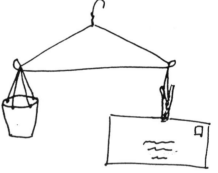

Figure 11–3.
How to make a simple postal scale. (A reproducible master for these instruction is included in the Appendix.)

Find a place to hang the balance where it can swing freely on a nail or hook. Experiment with bending the curved top of the hanger until the ends come to rest at equal heights.

To use your balance, clip the mail on one side and place pennies in the cup until the ends of the hanger are balanced again. Each penny weighs about one tenth of an ounce (0.1 oz.). Count the pennies to find the weight of your letter.

To raise the money needed for stamps and, if necessary, a scale, you can have a bake sale or undertake some other profit-making project. Stamps can be ordered by mail—the post office has special forms for this purpose. After the first batch of stamps has been purchased, the money taken in by selling them can be used to buy additional stamps as needed.

When the class post office is ready to open, supervision (perhaps from volunteer parents or older students) may be necessary at first, but students' motivation to learn the necessary skills will be high and they will work hard to do a good job.

Do let parents know when the class post office is open and encourage them to visit at those times.

IN SCHOOL AND/OR AT HOME: MORE PROBLEM-SOLVING ACTIVITIES

■ How many sheets of paper can one put in an envelope without going over an ounce?

■ If a ¼-ounce letter costs 29¢ to mail, how much does a letter twice as heavy cost? Do this problem for letters weighing ¾ ounce, 0.4 ounce, 0.5 ounce, 0.7 ounce, and so on.

■ Take ten letters and figure out how much it would cost to mail them. How much would you save by putting them all into one envelope?

■ Make a line graph of the cost of mailing a letter weighing 0.2 ounce, 0.4 ounce, 0.6 ounce, 0.8 ounce, 1.0 ounce, 1.2 ounces, etc. It will look like a set of steps. In fact, it is called a step function.

■ Find a catalog that gives a fax number. Would it be more expensive to mail a one-page order from your school to the catalog company or to fax it?

■ Encourage the children to invent mail-related problems for their classmates to solve. It takes just as much thinking to *create* a problem-solving question as it does to solve someone else's question.

Categorizing and Surveying Mail

As mentioned before, a great variety of mail comes to our homes almost every day—some of it most welcome, some of it thrown straight into the trash. There has been considerable publicity about problems created by steadily increasing volumes of unsolicited mail. Though not always welcome, this "junk mail," together with the regular mail, lends itself well to an exercise in sorting and categorizing.

IN SCHOOL: SORTING MAIL

With the help of friends and parents, collect a variety of mail: catalogs, magazines, advertising circulars, appeals for contributions, free introductory offers, and, if possible, envelopes from bills, personal letters, and greeting cards, as well as postcards.

Dear Parents,

Your children have probably been telling you about our classroom post office. They have worked hard to learn how to read a postal scale, how to weigh letters and figure out the right amount of postage, and how to make the correct change for their customers. The children have also learned how to order stamps from the post office. It would be great if your child could be in charge of putting the correct postage on your outgoing mail. Since a postal scale would be helpful, I'm including directions for a simple homemade scale in case you don't have one.

This week, the students will make a mail survey in school: they will learn about different types of mail and will practice sorting it into separate categories and charting the results by number and weight.

Next week, your child will be asked to categorize your incoming mail for a period of two weeks. He or she will bring home a form for recording the results of this daily mail survey. Please allow your child to count and weigh the pieces of mail in each category, and if necessary, help in recording the results.

The children have been enjoying the post office activities and have learned a lot of math. Encourage them to tell you about it!

Sincerely,

Figure 11–4. Letter to parents about learning to sort and classify mail. (A reproducible master for this form letter is included in the Appendix.)

When you have a sufficient quantity of mixed mail, have the children form groups: each group will get a packet of mixed mail to sort. When all the groups have sorted their mail, have the children compare their categories. Ask the groups to name their categories and then list these names on the board. Agreement on the different categories will have to be reached first.

AT HOME:
SURVEYING AND SORTING THE FAMILY MAIL

When the students have become familiar with all the different categories of mail, ask them to survey and categorize their own families' mail for one or two weeks. The sample letter in Figure 11–4 informs parents of the mail-related work done at school and asks them to help with a special homework project. It can be sent with a survey form (Figure 11–5) and a copy of the directions for making a balance scale (Figure 11–3).

FAMILY MAIL SURVEY

TYPE OF MAIL	NUMBER OF PIECES	WEIGHT
Bills	2	1 ½ oz.
Magazines and catalogs	3	1 lb.
Greeting cards	4	2 ¼ oz.
Advertising	9	4 oz.
Appeal for Money	1	3 oz.

Figure 11–5.
Family mail survey.
(A reproducible
master for this form
is included in the
Appendix.)

BACK IN SCHOOL:
ANALYZING THE RESULTS OF THE SURVEY

Here are some ways to use the data collected at home:

■ Ask the children to work in pairs to make a bar graph of the numbers and weights of the different categories of mail at each of their homes, using one color for number bars and another for weight bars.

■ Older children can also figure out what percentage of the total mail was bills, personal mail, advertising, and so on. Then they can make two pie graphs, one showing the distribution by weight and the other by number. Are the graphs similar?

■ Take a sampling of the mail received and pinpoint the zip codes of origin on a large map. Then:

Estimate the distance each piece of mail has traveled.

Estimate the minimum time it might have taken each piece to arrive at its destination.

A zip code book, available at the post office, would be a useful addition to your math resources.

Understanding Volume

Selecting and packing boxes for mailing is always a good test of our ability to judge volume. Trying to imagine the space that a collection of things will occupy when packed is not easy. In addition, some things require boxes with very large capacity simply because of their shape. Experience with matching contents to containers is necessary in order to develop the spatial sense needed to be a good judge of volume. It also lays the groundwork for understanding the measurement of volume.

IN SCHOOL: WHAT WILL FIT INTO THIS BOX?

Collect some boxes and cartons of different sizes to be filled with a variety of objects. Tennis balls, cans of food, books, and school supplies such as crayon boxes and masking tape will do fine. The children can contribute to this collection from items in their desks or cubbies. Make several piles of mixed objects and let the children pick the box they think will house the collection most efficiently. Then ask them to pack the objects into that box to check their estimate. This activity can be repeated by different groups of children: they can add or remove items, and try again to pick the best-sized box.

AT HOME: GAINING PRACTICE WITH JUDGING VOLUME

Whenever something has to be put into a box or container—whether it is mailing presents, storing clothes, putting old books in a carton to be sold or given away, or filling up a cookie jar—encourage parents to let their children pick the best size of available containers. Only practice will help children to become good at judging volume.

BACK IN SCHOOL: FROM PACKING TO MEASURING

Divide the class into small groups and supply each group with some small open boxes and just enough wooden or plastic cubes (all the same size) to fill the largest box. Ask each group to number the boxes and then write down on a slip of paper the number of the smallest box they think will hold all the cubes. After the students give you the paper slip, they can experiment packing the boxes with cubes to check their guesses. Were any guesses on the mark?

Tell the students that the *volume* of a box is the number of cubes it will hold and that the cubes are called *cubic units*. Ask them to find the volumes of the other boxes they have. Then give each group a new box, too large to be filled by the cubes they have. Can they figure out what its volume would be? Let each group present its estimate and explain how it was arrived at. It's possible that some will come up with the traditional formula for computing the volume of a rectangular box: length times width times height (using the edge of a cube as a unit of length). If not, save this for another time.

Surface Area and Volume of Boxes

If you have to go to the post office, buy a sampling of the mailing cartons sold there. Like the gift boxes in department stores, these come flattened and must be assembled. (Two examples are shown in Figure 11–6.) As you do this you can watch the two-dimensional object become three-dimensional and see the changing amount of space enclosed as the flattened box is shaped. Building and taking apart boxes is a good way to get a sense of the differences and relationships between two- and three-dimensional space.

Figure 11-6.
Drawings of
flattened boxes.

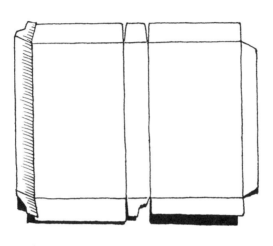

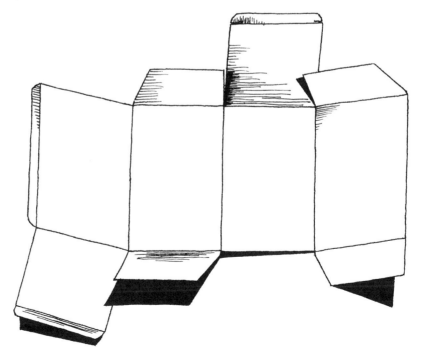

IN SCHOOL: BUILDING BOXES

Give each student a nine-by-twelve-inch sheet of light cardboard or tagboard with which to make an open box. The entire box must be made from this single sheet. Tape or glue may be used to hold it together. When students have finished, they should find the volumes of their boxes. For this purpose they can either use unit cubes or compute the volume using a formula.

Put the boxes on display, labeled with the volumes. Discuss the different methods students used for making the boxes. Also look for a relationship between the shape of the box and its volume. Which shapes seem to have the largest volumes? Which shapes, the smallest?

AT HOME: TAKING BOXES APART

Ask parents, ahead of time, to begin saving small food boxes and light cartons. When they have a sizeable collection the family can have a box-flattening session in which they carefully disassemble each box, taking care not to tear it. Then they should spread out their collection of disassembled boxes to see if any of them are similar in shape or in the design of their folds. These flattened boxes can be sorted into piles of similar shape and design. Students should bring to school a sample of each different shape found by the family.

BACK IN SCHOOL: THE MOST EFFICIENT BOX

Pool the flattened boxes from home and sort again, by similar shape. Add your boxes from the post office. Are they similar in design to any of the boxes from home? Let students reassemble the boxes if they want to. Which designs seem to produce the boxes that hold the most?

Repeat the box-making project from the in-school section, but this time challenge students to make a box with the largest possible volume from their one sheet of cardboard, using either a plan of their own or one of the designs in your collection. Again compare volumes and also surface areas of the resulting boxes. Can the students make any generalizations?

Apart from buying stamps and weighing letters and packages, most of us don't think of our incoming and outgoing mail as having rich mathematical potential. You may be surprised by this chapter's variety of mathematical ideas related to taking care of the mail. We have dealt only with traditional mail service. Think of the mathematical possibilities of such modern forms of mail as faxes, Federal Express, and electronic bulletin boards!

*Who made the
container with the
biggest volume?
A fifth-grade
experiment.*

With a 9x12 paper we wanted to build a container that would hold the greatest volume of rice. We all made boxes out of tagboard. Then we filled them with rice and weighed the rice against each other. We used a balance scale and whoevers went down furthest on the scale won. We did this to see whose invention held the most volume.

Not all of the inventions were boxes. The best design was a canoe shape and these were a few cylinders and ice cream cone shapes as well.

Brady

12
Cars and Travel

A good deal of day-to-day mathematics has to do with getting from place to place, whether by automobile or bicycle or on foot. Some of the following investigations can be undertaken by every child or family; others are appropriate only for families with automobiles. Since cars are part of almost everyone's environment, the children of families without cars may well be as interested as the other students. Ways to include these children will be suggested later in this chapter.

Taking Traffic Counts

One way to gain an appreciation of the volume and variety of traffic on our streets is to take a traffic count. To do this, children will have to learn how to keep track of passing vehicles by tallying.

IN SCHOOL:
KEEPING A TALLY OF PASSING VEHICLES

If your classroom windows face a street with traffic, small groups of kids can easily take a count at different times of the day. Let the children decide how long they should spend counting. After a while, they may want to change their original time limit. Five minutes may not be enough time for a tally in a quiet street, while fifteen minutes may be too long for a very busy street. Children will learn more if they have to come to the right decision by trial and error.

Start by having the children count all the passing vehicles. Later, they may want to make different categories of vehicles. There are many possibilities. They could, for instance, list cars, vans, trucks, bicycles, and motorcycles. Groups of four or five children could go to different locations, count the same vehicles, and then compare their results; or the various groups could each count different categories of vehicles on the same street. Results can then be combined in one chart or graph.

If you cannot see any traffic from your classroom window or from any other spot in your school, you will have to go out into the streets. Perhaps an aide or a parent volunteer can take small groups of kids. A piece of stiff cardboard and a clothespin with a spring can be used to make a good clipboard (see Figure 12–1). The paper attached to the clipboard should list the different categories of vehicles to be counted and leave plenty of room for the tallies.

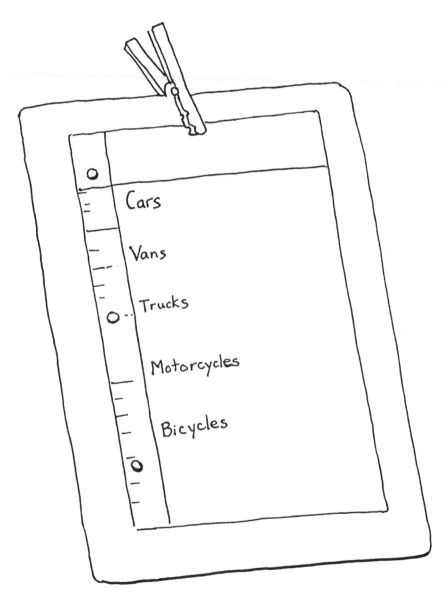

Figure 12–1.
A clipboard for tallying traffic.

If groups of children take counts at different times of day and on different days of the week, they will be able to compare results. What conclusions can be drawn? Let the children study the counts in small groups and see what answers they come up with.

AT HOME: A TRAFFIC COUNT ON MY STREET

Send home a blank tally sheet (see Figure 12–2) and ask the children to take a count of the traffic outside their homes or on a nearby street. Be sure the children record at what time of day and on what day of the week they made their count.

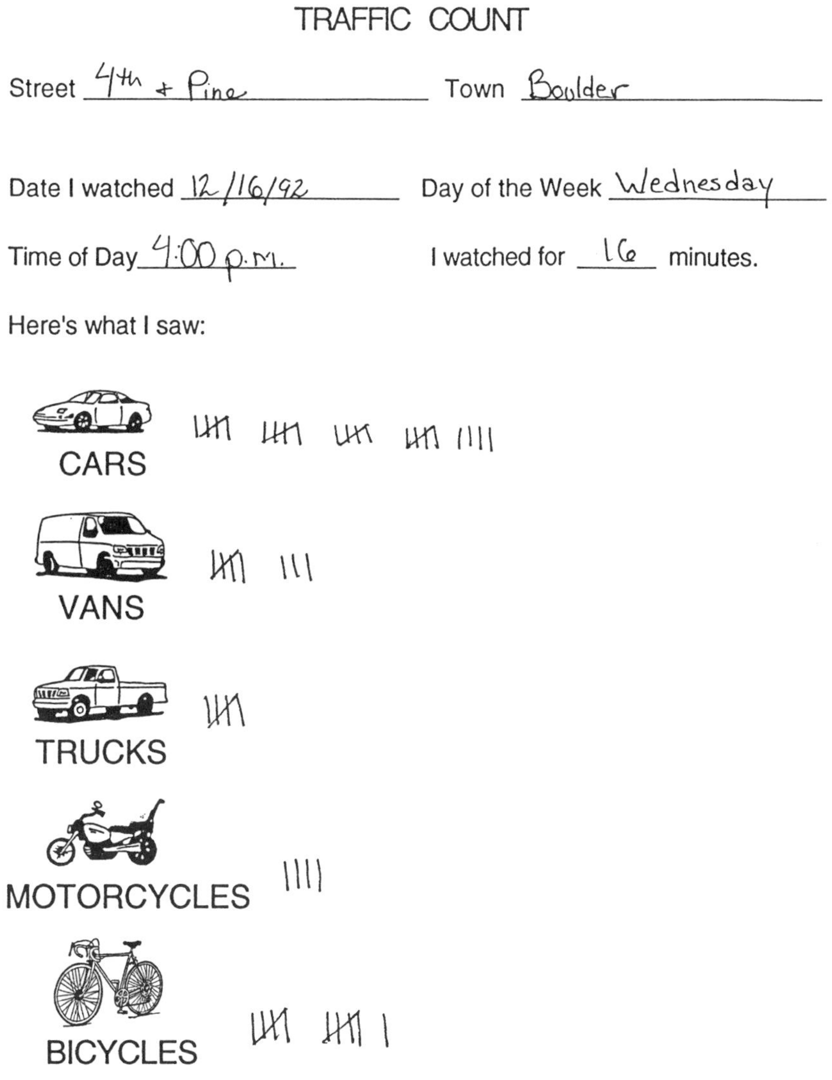

TRAFFIC COUNT

Street _4th + Pine_   Town _Boulder_

Date I watched _12/16/92_   Day of the Week _Wednesday_

Time of Day _4:00 p.m._   I watched for _16_ minutes.

Here's what I saw:

CARS   � LHT LHT LHT LHT IIII

VANS   LHT III

TRUCKS   LHT

MOTORCYCLES   IIII

BICYCLES   LHT LHT I

Figure 12–2. Traffic tally sheet. (A reproducible master for this form is included in the Appendix.)

BACK IN SCHOOL: MAKING CHARTS AND GRAPHS

When the surveys are brought back to school, children will have more information to discuss, compare, and graph. By sorting their record sheets by street, for instance, they will be able to investigate questions like:

- How much does the volume of traffic differ on the streets where children live?
- Which streets have the most truck traffic?
- Do weekdays and weekends show different traffic patterns?

Learning to tally, classify, make graphs of tallied results, and interpret the graphs are useful skills to master. Just as important, however, are the questions children may raise as they think about such a project. *Who* takes traffic counts? *Why* are traffic counts taken? If the Highway Department wants a traffic count on a particular street, do they send people out to count the cars or do they use different methods? Invite someone from the Highway Department to visit your class so that the children can share their traffic surveys, ask questions they have previously discussed and listed, and gain additional traffic-related knowledge from an expert.

Road Sign Geometry

It's important for children to understand that road signs have a purpose. Why and where, for instance, do speed limits change? Why are drivers warned of sharp curves or icy roads? Why can heavy trucks not go over certain bridges? By paying attention to the location of different signs, children are challenged to think and to make connections between the road terrain and the various signs that are placed there. Knowing what the different shapes and colors of road signs mean helps drivers to see the messages of the road signs as quickly as possible.

IN SCHOOL:
THE SHAPES AND COLORS OF ROAD SIGNS

Try to get a few driver's manuals from your local motor vehicle bureau—they have reproductions of road signs as well as other interesting information.

Whether children are walking, biking, or riding in a car or a bus, they will see road signs. Some of the shapes, colors, and purposes of road signs can be learned by even the youngest students. For instance:

An octagon always means a full stop.

A triangle means yield.

A round sign means a railroad crossing.

A pentagon indicates a school zone and/or school crossing.

There are other highway signs with different shapes:

■ *Warning signs* are diamond shaped and yellow. They alert the driver to existing or possible hazards on the road. They may include words (like "Narrow Bridge") or pictures (a car and skid marks or a truck going downhill, for instance) or lines (indicating curves, intersections, or side roads).

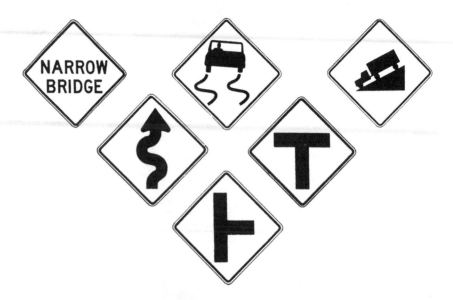

■ *Regulatory signs* are white vertical rectangles with black letters. These signs tell you what you must or must not do:

■ *Guide signs* are green squares and horizontal rectangles with white letters. They give directional information such as announcing exits from highways or pointing the driver to bike and hiking trails.

■ *Service signs* are blue and indicate service facilities such as campgrounds, picnic areas, public telephones, restaurants and grocery stores, hotels and motels, gas stations, and hospitals.

Children enjoy browsing through a drivers' manual to study the different shapes and colors of road signs. They can also make their own road signs—copied from the manual or from actual road signs they have seen—to use in the "block area" or to display in the classroom.

AT HOME: LOOKING FOR MORE ROAD SIGNS

Signs on the open road.

Ask the children to be on the lookout for new road signs they can make to add to the existing collection. Suggest that parents, if they have the time, take a special drive on a weekend to find new and interesting signs: the weight and height limits for trucks by bridges and tunnels, warnings to truck drivers to shift into low gear on steep downhill grades, notifications of deer and cattle crossings, high wind warnings, and so on. Parents can help their children spot and reproduce signs

they see and take note of where they are placed. Understanding the reasons behind the rules will help children to appreciate as well as to obey the information on warning and regulatory signs when they themselves become drivers.

Parents can also add signs *they* have seen on their travels by bus or car. If children have their own ideas for additional road signs, they should be encouraged to design them.

BACK IN SCHOOL: SORTING ROAD SIGNS BY SHAPE AND FUNCTION

When you have a good-sized collection of signs, ask the children to sort them by shape or function. After classifying the signs, children can compare their categories with those listed in the drivers' manual. Are all warning signs diamond shaped? Do all green rectangular signs have similar messages? This will give children a chance to see shapes, symbols, and numbers being used to communicate important information.

Road Maps and Symbols

Road maps contain a lot of useful mathematical information. Although they are no longer available free of charge at gas stations, you can usually get one or two free road maps of your state at the local Chamber of Commerce. Many children enjoy looking at maps and are eager to learn to read them (see the drawing in Figure 12–3). In the process they can become good map readers.

SCHOOL PROJECT: LEARNING TO INTERPRET SYMBOLS ON ROAD MAPS

Maps have many symbols. Show the children how to read the key or legend at the side or bottom of a map, which explains the different symbols. To give children practice in reading the symbols, see if they can find state capitals, cities of a certain size, parks and recreation areas, interstate highways, gravel roads, tunnels, and so on. Then divide the class into smaller groups and give each group a map to study. What can they learn about the region shown on the map? Help them get started by distributing a list of questions. For instance:

- What states are shown on this map?
- Where are the boundaries?

- How can you tell the difference between an interstate highway and a country road?
- What different symbols are used for towns and cities?
- Can you tell what part of the state is most densely populated?
- Can you find lakes? rivers? forests? deserts? mountains?

Ask each group to make up three additional questions that can be answered by studying the maps and map keys. Groups can then trade questions.

Some children may enjoy inventing map symbols that they can add to local city maps: favorite playgrounds or restaurants, best streets for skate boards or bike riding, and so on. Some may want to make up imaginary maps with invented symbols, while others might enjoy making maps of places in books or stories they have read.

A good way to introduce younger children to maps is to get an aerial survey photograph from your local planning department, one showing a familiar part of your community (like your school).

Figure 12–3.
A young man
directs a family trip.

"I can see my house!"

Children will be able to recognize landmarks and even find their own homes on these large-scale photomaps.

Commercial maps have large grids marked with numbers and letters at the four sides. The grids divide the map into sections, which are named by these numbers and letters (coordinates), to help you find a particular spot. Distribute identical maps to groups of students. Then let one student at a time give the coordinates of familiar cities or towns on this map. See whether the others can guess which city or town he or she had in mind. This activity will provide practice in locating a point with the aid of a grid, a skill that will be needed later in coordinate graphing.

Scale

Maps are good for introducing older children to the topic of scale. To help children understand that maps can be drawn to different scales, try to get several maps that include your state. On a state map, one inch may equal eighteen miles; on a map of the Western United States, one inch may equal fifty miles; on a map of the United States, one inch may equal ninety miles. The idea that a map can be made to any scale is important, but not easy to grasp.

IN SCHOOL: MAPPING THE CLASSROOM

Divide the class into small groups to measure and make a map of the classroom. All the groups will use half-inch graph paper for their room maps, but half the class will measure the room in feet using the scale one-half inch equals one foot, while the other half will measure it in yards using the scale one-half inch equals one yard. When all the groups have finished, have the students compare their maps. Why are they not the same size? Allow plenty of time for discussion so that the children can arrive at a beginning understanding of scale.

As an optional extension of the map work, you can offer interested students graph paper with smaller and larger grids (one centimeter, one-quarter inch, three-quarter inch, one inch). Have them choose a size and ask them to speculate what size the room map will be when transferred onto the different grid.

AT HOME: MAPPING A ROOM TO SCALE

Ask students to map their favorite room, using a scale previously agreed on and graph paper you supply. If they or other family members want to rearrange a room, the children can make a floor plan and cut out furniture drawn to scale, so different room arrangements can be tried out. If a student's family has a house plan or blueprint, the room map can be compared to it. Is the scale the same?

BACK IN SCHOOL: COMPARING ROOM SIZES

Children can bring their room maps back to school and display them on a bulletin board. Cover the children's names on the maps and label them with numbers or letters. Let everyone guess which room is the largest. You can make a simple graph showing how many children "voted" for the different rooms. After estimating, children can count the squares on the graph paper to determine the actual area of each room. Then they can compare the room sizes, as well as discuss what factors may have led them to make mistaken estimates.

The Family Car: Rate of Gas Consumption

Gasoline consumption, expressed in miles per gallon, is one of the most familiar examples of *rate*. Learning to compute the rate of gasoline usage will give students a better grasp of this concept.

Teachers are urged to be sensitive to the feelings of children whose families do not own a car. They might ask these children if a family friend or relative has a car that can be used for some of the activities; there might be a member of the school staff willing to "adopt" a youngster for the duration of the car curriculum; or "noncar" children can pair up with "car children" to work together on some activities.

IN SCHOOL: WHAT ARE MILES PER GALLON?

The calculations involved in figuring out miles per gallon are not really complicated once the concept is clearly understood. First, children have to learn to understand what "miles per gallon" means. Be sure they are clear about the following:

> **1.** How long is one mile? Walk one mile with your class or point out two familiar landmarks, like home and school, that are one mile apart, in order to give the students some sense of the length of a mile.
> **2.** "A gallon" refers to a gallon of gasoline. Bring in an empty gallon can or jug so the children can *see* how much gasoline is being talked about when "miles per gallon" are mentioned.
> **3.** Label the gallon jug "32 miles" to emphasize that if a car "gets" thirty-two miles per gallon, it means that this car uses up (or burns) one gallon of gasoline while being driven for thirty-two miles. Fill the jug with water and pour out one-half cup ($1/32$ of a gallon) to show the amount of gasoline consumed in driving one mile. Give groups of students a road atlas and ask them to find two towns or other landmarks in the vicinity which are approximately thirty-two miles apart.

Next, help the children understand how to keep track of a car's mileage and gas consumption. Tell them the odometer reading on your car the last two times you filled your tank and the number of gallons of gas you bought at the second filling. With this information, groups of students can work on computing your gasoline consumption in miles per gallon. Let them explain how they arrived at their answer. When a valid method has been identified, help them write it up. For example:

> ■ First, you must keep track of a car's mileage and gas consumption:
>   Read the odometer when you fill up the car's tank.
>   Read the odometer again the next time the tank is filled.
>   Record the amount of gas put into the tank the second time.
> ■ Then, you can calculate how many miles per gallon the car got:
>   How many miles were driven? (Difference between the two odometer readings.)
>   How much gasoline was used? (The amount it took to fill the car's tank when you took the second odometer reading.)
>   How many miles per gallon did your car get? (Divide the number of miles driven by the amount of gasoline purchased.)

For example, if you drove 265 miles and used 8 gallons of gas, your car got 33.125 miles per gallon (265 ÷ 8 = 33.125). Students are more likely to remember a procedure like this if they work it through themselves and then write down the steps.

AT HOME: KEEPING TRACK OF GAS CONSUMPTION

When children feel comfortable with computing miles per gallon, send home a note asking parents to help their kids keep track of the family car's mileage and gas consumption over a period of time (see Figure 12–4). Attach a sample record sheet (Figure 12–5) to the letter that children can copy into a notebook.

Briefly discuss the information asked for on the chart, especially the column headed "driving conditions." What might this mean? You can mention driving in the city, on a flat highway, on a gravel country

Figure 12–4.

Letter to parents about keeping track of gas consumption. (A reproducible master for this form letter is included in the Appendix.)

Dear Parents,

Have your children been talking about their most recent math study—calculating the rate of a car's gas consumption? In preparation for this assignment, we have been discussing the meaning of the term "miles per gallon": we have walked a mile, looked at gallon jugs and cans, and studied area maps to find familiar towns that are approximately thirty miles apart. The children are beginning to understand how much gas is used by a car that "gets" thirty miles per gallon (mpg).

We've practiced how to keep track of and calculate a car's mileage and gas consumption, and we've also talked about road and driving conditions that may influence gas consumption—in the city or on highways; on flat, hilly, paved, or gravel roads; in good or bad weather; in light or heavy traffic.

The children now need practice in a real situation and are looking forward to keeping track of their family car's rate of gas consumption. I've enclosed a chart for you to use for this purpose, as well as directions that outline the method the students used when making these calculations in school. I hope they will be able to practice with you and that everyone will enjoy this family project. Records like these can be most useful when you take longer family trips, and your children will gain valuable skills keeping these records.

Good luck!

GASOLINE CONSUMPTION

Date	Odometer Reading	Number of Miles Driven	Amount of Gas Used	Miles Per Gallon	Cost of One Gallon	Total Cost	Driving Conditions
11/24	38,156	—	—	—	—	—	————
12/3	38,437	281	9.36g.	30.02	$1.29	$12.07	Mostly flat Interstate
12/10	38,667	230	9.02g.	25.50	$1.28	$11.55	City - ice and Snow on road
12/22	38,931	264	9.60g.	27.50	$1.27	$12.19	City and Mountain Roads

Figure 12–5. Gasoline consumption chart. (A reproducible master for this form, as well as instructions for using it, is included in the Appendix.)

road, on a mountain road, and so on. Do students think it makes a difference on what kind of road you drive? Leave this an open question to be discussed again later, after the students have kept records for a few weeks.

BACK IN SCHOOL: WHAT AFFECTS GAS CONSUMPTION?

When students have kept records for a period of time, let them talk about where their families were driving and then ask them the following questions:

■ Does it matter *where* you drive? Did your car use gasoline at the same rate when it was driven around town, in the mountains, or on the interstate?
■ Does it matter *how fast* you drive? Will driving at sixty-five miles per hour use the same amount of gasoline as driving at fifty miles per hour?

■ Does it matter if you *stop and start* frequently? Do stop signs and traffic lights in the city affect gas consumption?

■ Does the road surface—dirt or asphalt—have any effect on gas consumption?

See what ideas the children come up with. Some experiments in the school gym might be helpful here. Ask the children to:

■ Run the length of the gym without stopping, and then run back stopping and starting again every ten feet. Which took more energy?

■ Run around the gym as fast as they can and then at a somewhat slower speed. Which made them more tired?

■ Push a heavy object across the gym floor. What takes more energy: to get it moving initially, or to keep it moving once it is started?

Also ask the children how running uphill compares with running on a flat road. Experiencing these things with their own bodies will make it easier for children to understand some of the factors that influence gas consumption.

Planning Trips: Time, Distance, and Speed

When traveling, we are constantly raising questions involving time, distance, and speed. How long will it take to get to the beach? How far can I go by dinnertime? What's the speed limit on this road? If children could be their parents' partners in making estimates and decisions, they would have wonderful opportunities to encounter mathematical questions and to begin to get a sense of how time, distance, and speed are related.

IN SCHOOL: PLANNING IMAGINARY TRIPS

Before school vacations, students can choose five or six places around the country that they might like to visit. Working with a road map, individual groups can plot a route from their hometown to the place of their choice. After the various routes have been decided, the children can figure out the total distance and estimate how long it would take them to get there at different driving speeds. If it is a long trip, children can also decide where they might want to stop overnight and how many miles they would be driving each day.

HELPFUL HINTS FOR TEACHERS

Time, Distance, and Speed

Estimating travel time raises the question of speed—a concept children often have trouble with if it is taught abstractly. Speed becomes more understandable when it is connected with modes of transportation the children know well. How far could they travel in an hour if they were walking, riding a bike, driving on the highway, or flying? Since most people can walk about three miles in an hour, we could say walking speed is three miles per hour (mph). On a bike you might travel 10 mph; in a car on the highway, 65 mph; in a plane, 300 mph. When you've established these rates of speed, ask how far one could walk, ride, travel by car, or fly in two hours, three hours, four hours, etc. Can the children make a rule for figuring out how far you could travel in any number of hours?

To make clear the relationship between time, distance, and speed, look at what happens if one of these stays the same. It is easy to understand, for example, that you will get to a place in *less time* if you drive *faster*. If that place is 120 miles away and you are traveling 60 miles per hour, it will take two hours, but at 40 miles per hour it will take three hours. Changing the speed changes the time, too.

AT HOME: HELPING TO PLAN FAMILY TRIPS

Let parents know that their children have been working on planning imaginary trips. Tell them about the children's map-reading skills and about their understanding of the concept of speed. Encourage parents to let the children participate in the planning of family trips and suggest that they consult the children to solve questions like:

- How long will it take us to get to _____ if our average speed on this country road is fifty miles per hour?
- If we want to stop driving for the day in another three hours, how far will we get, driving at a speed of sixty-five miles per hour? Is there a town about that far away where we can spend the night?

Helping their parents plan trips and being able to estimate time or distance on long car trips are ways for your students to see the importance and usefulness of math outside school.

Keeping Track of Car-Related Facts and Figures

Some children might enjoy keeping track of car-related facts and figures, both at home and on trips away from home. Suggest that parents give their kids a special car notebook in which they can record things like the following:

At home
- Mileage and date when the oil is changed.
- Mileage and date when the tires are rotated.
- Date on which the antifreeze was last checked, as well as the temperature to which it was effective.
- Correct tire pressure, front and rear wheels.
- Any other things that get checked at regular intervals.

On trips
- Number of miles driven—recorded daily, when the gas tank is filled, between cities, or any other way that makes sense.
- Amount of gas used—recorded whenever gas is purchased.
- Cost of gas. Prices will vary, so children should record price per gallon as well as total cost each time gas is purchased.

At the end of trips
- Total number of miles driven.
- Total cost of gas.
- Average cost of one gallon of gas (total cost of gas divided by total number of gallons purchased).
- Average rate of gasoline consumption (total number of miles driven divided by total number of gallons purchased).

Since many of us spend a great deal of time driving or riding in a car, we may as well use this time productively. A car curriculum like the one suggested in this chapter could easily last an entire semester. We have touched on a relatively small number of possible car-related math activities. We hope that you, your students, and their families will come up with many additional ideas.

Afterword

Two main themes run through these pages: (1) elementary mathematics instruction should emphasize meaningful everyday activities from children's lives and (2) parents should be helped to value their own knowledge of math, share this knowledge with their children, and become active participants in the home components of the everyday math curriculum.

Some of you may find this a welcome new approach to teaching mathematics; others may need a little time before feeling ready to try some of the activities recommended here. However, if the teachers we worked with are at all typical, it probably won't take long before you begin to feel comfortable with everyday math. The teachers we've worked with selected various projects, tried them, and then reported how much they and the children enjoyed the work. In almost all cases, they had additional ideas, derived from their own thinking and doing, as well as from their students' questions and comments.

We hope that you too will find the activities interesting and challenging, and that working with parents and children will stimulate your thinking about this different way of teaching math. Feel free to improvise and invent as you go along, adding your ideas to those you find here.

As you browse through the chapters to select appropriate projects for your students, you will see that our daily routines provide us with an endless number of mathematical opportunities. Instead of asking yourself, What am I going to do in math next week? you may be wondering when you will be able to try out all these new ideas. Lack of time may be a problem, but you are not likely ever to run out of things to do in your everyday math curriculum!

References

BOOKS AND ARTICLES

Blocksma, Mary. 1989. *Reading the Numbers: A Survival Guide to the Measurements, Numbers, and Sizes Encountered in Everyday Life.* New York: Penguin.

Board on Mathematical Sciences and Mathematical Sciences Education Board, National Research Council. 1989. *Everybody Counts: A Report to the Nation on the Future of Mathematics Education.* Washington DC: National Academy Press.

Dewey, John. [1900, 1902] 1956. *The Child and the Curriculum* and *The School and Society.* Chicago: University of Chicago Press.

Gailey, Stavroula. 1993. "The Mathematics–Children's Literature Connection." *Arithmetic Teacher* 40(5):13.

Griffiths, Rachel, and Margaret Clyne. 1991. *Books You Can Count On.* Portsmouth, NH: Heinemann.

Gamberg, Ruth, Winniefred Kwak, Meredith Hutchings, and Judy Altheim. 1988. *Learning and Loving It: Theme Studies in the Classroom.* Portsmouth, NH: Heinemann.

Hardy, G. H. [1945] 1969. *A Mathematician's Apology.* London: Cambridge University Press.

Leeb-Lundberg, Kristina. 1970. "Kindergarten Mathematics Laboratory—Nineteenth-Century Fashion." *Arithmetic Teacher* 17(5): 372–85.

Maier, Eugene. 1977. "Folk Math." *Instructor Magazine* 86(6):84–92.

National Council of Teachers of Mathematics. 1989. *Curriculum and Evaluation Standards for School Mathematics.* Reston, VA: The Council.

Parker, Tom. 1984. *In One Day.* Boston: Houghton Mifflin.

Whitin, David, and Sandra Wilde. 1993. *Read Any Good Math Lately? Children's Books for Mathematical Learning, K–6.* Portsmouth, NH: Heinemann.

COMPUTER PROGRAM

The Marketplace 1984. St. Paul: Minnesota Educational Computing Consortium.

APPENDIX

Reproducible Blank Forms and Sample Letters

THIS LETTER IS ABOUT OUR EVERYDAY MATH PROGRAM

Dear Parents,

This year I want to help your children see how mathematics is used in everyday life, so that they can learn new skills in practical, enjoyable situations. The math you use at home will be an essential part of this program. It won't take any special expertise on your part—just your willingness to share what you already know and do every day.

Please come to a meeting that I have scheduled to give you an opportunity to find out more about our program. We will meet in Room _____ at _____ p.m. on _____ .

Sincerely,

Your name _____

Your child's name _____

How do you feel about being part of a home/school math program? _____

_____

Do you have any special suggestions for this program?

_____

_____

_____

Do you have any interests or talents that involve math and that you would be

willing to share with the class? _____

If so, what are they? _____

_____

Please add any other comments or suggestions you would like to make.

_____

_____

_____

Thank you for coming, and thanks for your help!

NAME _____

THEN AND NOW: HOW OFTEN DID I EAT?

NOW

KIND OF MEAL						
TIME						

I eat _____ times a day.

WHEN I WAS A BABY

KIND OF MEAL						
TIME						

I was fed _____ times a day.

NAME _____

THEN AND NOW: HOW LONG DID I SLEEP?

Now I go to sleep at _____ and wake up at _____ .

I sleep _____ hours each night.

When I was a baby I slept more often.

I went to sleep at	and woke up at	I slept
_____	_____	_____ hours
_____	_____	_____ hours
_____	_____	_____ hours
_____	_____	_____ hours
_____	_____	_____ hours
_____	_____	_____ hours

I slept _____ hours each day.

THIS LETTER IS ABOUT LEARNING MATH IN THE SUPERMARKET

Dear Parents,

We are trying to see in how many different ways we can use the supermarket to study math. We want to start with matching, an important early math activity. Even before children can read, they can recognize products by their labels. I would like the children to learn how to find things in the supermarket by taking labels removed from cans or cut from boxes and matching them with the identical labels on products displayed on the shelves. I hope that your youngsters will soon be able to help you with your grocery shopping!

Please send us some empty cans and food boxes (two of each individual product) to make a display in the classroom so that the children can practice matching. Thank you for your help.

Sincerely,

NAME _____

WHAT I COUNTED IN THE SUPERMARKET

Name of the Store_____

Day of the Week _____ Time of Day_____

WHAT I COUNTED	HOW MANY
_____	_____
_____	_____
_____	_____
_____	_____
_____	_____
_____	_____
_____	_____
_____	_____

NAME _____

SHAPES I FOUND IN THE SUPERMARKET

WHAT I FOUND	ITS SHAPE
_____	_____
_____	_____
_____	_____
_____	_____
_____	_____
_____	_____
_____	_____
_____	_____
_____	_____
_____	_____

THIS LETTER IS ABOUT PRACTICING COUNTING IN THE KITCHEN

Dear Parents,

We've been practicing counting objects at school. You can help your child get more practice if you encourage him or her to count things in the course of your daily activities. In the kitchen, for instance, children can count the number of

- spoons in the drawer
- items you unpack from grocery bags
- ingredients used in a recipe
- utensils on the dinner table
- plates or glasses taken from the dishwasher
  and so on.

Don't worry if your child makes mistakes like skipping a number or counting one object twice and another not at all. Try not to correct these at this stage of counting—such mistakes are quite common. Learning to count is a lengthy and complicated process, and only practice, time, and experience will teach your child to do it correctly.

See how many things you can find to count—in the kitchen and in the rest of your home!

Sincerely,

NAME _____

TO GET READY FOR WRITING MULTIPLICATION STORIES WE ARE LOOKING FOR OBJECTS WHICH REGULARLY COME IN SETS OF A CERTAIN SIZE. YOUR KITCHEN IS AN EXCELLENT PLACE TO FIND SUCH THINGS (LIKE FORKS WITH FOUR TINES EACH OR GRAHAM CRACKERS IN PACKAGES OF 8).

PLEASE HELP YOUR CHILD TO LOOK FOR MORE EXAMPLES AND TO NAME OR DRAW SOME OF THESE IN THE BOXES BELOW. FEEL FREE TO INCLUDE OBJECTS OR SETS FROM OTHER PARTS OF YOUR HOME AS WELL.

NAME _____

FAMILY FOOD QUESTION

How much _____ does our family eat (or drink) in a year?

    or

How many _____ do our family eat (or drink) in a year?

WRITE THE FOOD OR DRINK OF YOUR CHOICE IN ONE OR BOTH OF THE QUESTIONS ABOVE. TAKE YOUR QUESTION(S) HOME AND TRY TO ESTIMATE AN ANSWER WITH YOUR FAMILY. ASK OTHERS IN YOUR FAMILY FOR ANY INFORMATION YOU NEED BUT DON'T HAVE. ALSO ASK THEM HOW THEY WOULD ESTIMATE THE ANSWER. IT'S O.K. TO USE A CALCULATOR.

Our answer to this question is _____.

This is how we found it:

Here are some other questions we would like to answer:

THIS LETTER IS ABOUT LEARNING FRACTIONS IN THE KITCHEN

Dear Parents,

You may already have heard from your children that we are studying fractions. In school, we try to use phrases like "one third," "three fourths," "one and two fifths," and so on, as often as possible. It helps children to become familiar with these concepts.

We would really appreciate it if you could try to "talk fractions" with your kids whenever you are dividing up food. When cutting up a pizza, you can talk about slicing it into eighths. Some apple corers also cut apples into twelve equal sections and these can be referred to as twelfths. If four people are to share the apple, each one will get one quarter or three twelfths. Children can be asked to divide a banana into quarters, a peeled orange into fifths, or a loaf cake into sixths. Give your children time to find their own strategies for dividing different shapes; this will help them see which fractions are relatively easy to section off and which are more difficult. How do you cut a pizza into fifths or tenths?

It would also be most helpful if your kids could assist you with any measuring you have to do when preparing meals. A set of measuring spoons and cups would make a great gift when children are learning about fractions. Your children could experiment with a couple of large bowls, a set of measuring cups and spoons, and some salt or cornmeal, and gain useful practice for future measuring jobs.

Thank you so much for your cooperation.

Sincerely,

FRACTION EXPERIMENTS -- FIRST DAY

Ask someone in your family to show you the fractional markings on a one-cup measure. Ask that person to help you while you do the following:

Measure 1/4 cup of water and pour it into a glass.

Next measure 1/2 cup of water and leave it in the cup.

Pour the water from the glass back into the measuring cup.

Read the marking at the water level.

How much water is in the cup? _____

$$\frac{1}{2} + \frac{1}{4} = \underline{\quad\quad}$$

Experiment with the measuring cup to find two more addition facts using fractions.

Write them here.

_____

_____

FRACTION EXPERIMENTS -- SECOND DAY

Get out the measuring cup again. Ask someone in your family to keep count as you measure $\frac{1}{3}$ cup of water and pour it into a glass four times.

Then measure the water in the glass.

How much is there? _____

$$4 \times \frac{1}{3} = \text{\underline{\hspace{2cm}}}$$

Ask your partner to measure out $\frac{1}{4}$ cup of water 3 times. Write a new multiplication sentence to describe the result.

_____

Measure out $\frac{1}{4}$ cup of water 2 times. Write a multiplication sentence to describe the result.

_____

FRACTION EXPERIMENTS -- THIRD DAY

Get your measuring partner to watch while you pour $1\frac{1}{2}$ cups of water into a container. Divide the water evenly between two identical glasses. Measure the water in one glass. How much is there?

$$\frac{1}{2} \text{ of } 1\frac{1}{2} \text{ is _____.}$$

$$\text{Write} \quad \frac{1}{2} \times 1\frac{1}{2} = \text{_____}$$

Now watch while your partner does the same thing, starting with $\frac{2}{3}$ cup of water.

$$\frac{1}{2} \times \frac{2}{3} = \text{_____}$$

Do it once more, starting with $1\frac{1}{3}$ cups of water.

$$\frac{1}{2} \times 1\frac{1}{3} = \text{_____}$$

FRACTION EXPERIMENTS -- FOURTH DAY

Cut an apple, a pizza, or something else you are eating into eight equal pieces. Eat one of the eighths.

How many eighths are left? _____.

$$1 - \frac{1}{8} = \underline{\hspace{1cm}}$$

Put six of the remaining $\frac{1}{8}$ pieces on a plate and let two members of your family take one apiece. Ask them to guess what fraction of the whole will be left.

What fraction <u>is</u> left on the plate? _____

$$\frac{6}{8} - \frac{2}{8} = \underline{\hspace{1cm}}$$

Do you have enough of the eighths left over to make one half? _____

If so, how many eighths did it take to make the half? _____

$$\frac{1}{2} \div \frac{1}{8} = \underline{\hspace{1cm}}$$

NAME _____

HOW MANY CUPS?

ONE HALF PINT _____ CUPS

ONE PINT _____ CUPS

ONE QUART _____ CUPS

ONE HALF GALLON _____ CUPS

ONE GALLON _____ CUPS

THIS LETTER IS ABOUT DOUBLING A RECIPE

Dear Parents,

Kitchen-related mathematics seems to have no end! We've been wondering what happens when you double a bread or cake recipe. Each student will bring home a copy of the same recipe. However, since we like variety, feel free to substitute your own favorite bread or cake recipe for this experiment. It will make our tasting party more interesting.

Please help your child when necessary but let him or her try to figure out what to do even if you know that the result may not be perfect. We all learn from our mistakes! Thanks for your help and your patience.

Sincerely,

ASSIGNMENT

The following recipe serves four people. Double it, so that it will serve eight. Please write out the entire new recipe, including the size of pan you used, oven temperature, and baking time. Ask someone in your family to be available to help you with this project.

Please do this assignment by _____ and, if possible, bring a sample of your baking to school.

CORN BREAD

Sift these together:

3/4 cup cornmeal   2 tablespoons sugar
1/2 cup flour   1/4 teaspoon salt
2 teaspoons baking powder

Combine these and beat them:

1 egg   2 tablespoons melted
1/2 cup milk   margarine

Now do this:

Turn on the oven and set it to 425 degrees
Grease a loaf pan (9" x 4")
Combine the two mixtures, stir until they are well blended, and pour them into the greased pan.
Bake the mixture for 20 to 25 minutes.

A VOLUME EXPERIMENT TO DO AT HOME

Gathering and Preparing Materials

Collect an assortment of bottles, bowls, and plastic food and storage containers from your kitchen.

Remove or cover all labels on the containers so that the measurements cannot be seen.

Add a funnel to the collection to help you with pouring liquids.

Doing the Experiment - Part I

Line up all the containers by increasing volume: Start with the one that you think will hold the least amount of liquid and continue lining up containers until you get to the one that you think will hold the most.

Number the containers in order from the one you think is smallest to the one you think is largest.

Doing the Experiment - Part II

For the second part of the experiment you need a pitcher of water with a few drops of food coloring in it. This will make it easier to see the water level if you are using transparent containers.

Try to establish the true order of volume of your containers—from the smallest to the largest one—by pouring water from one to the other.

Compare the new order with your estimated order.

Describe your results in writing: How correct were your estimates when you lined up all the containers by increasing volume?

Try to figure out where a quart—and if possible a liter—fit into the sequence.

Were there any surprises when you started to measure the containers? Did some of the shapes of bottles or containers mislead you?

Did you observe anything that might improve your future volume estimates?

Do you have questions or discoveries to share with the class?

NAME_____

COST OF SOFT DRINKS

AT RESTAURANTS IN _____
(YOUR CITY OR TOWN)

RESTAURANT	SIZE	FLUID OUNCES	COST	COST PER FL. OZ

NAME _____

FAMILY   PIZZA   FAVORITES

Our family likes _____'s pizza.

This pizza is available in the following sizes:

SIZE	DIAMETER	COST
_____	_____	_____
_____	_____	_____
_____	_____	_____
_____	_____	_____

Cashier trainee's name _____

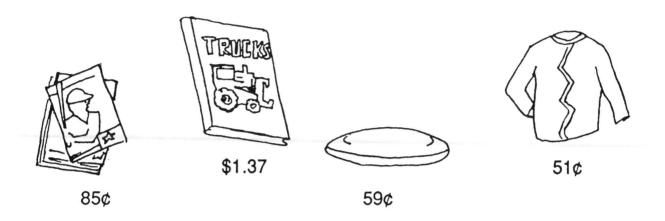

$1.37

51¢

85¢

59¢

What coins would you give each customer in change?

1) Rada wants the baseball cards. She gives you a dollar.

2) Nathan gives you a dollar and two quarters for the book.

3) Liu hands you three quarters. He wants the frisbee.

4) Karen would like to buy the doll sweater. She gives you two quarters and
   a dime.

THIS LETTER IS ABOUT LEARNING TO SAVE MONEY

Dear Parents,

In class, we've been working on planning for saving and spending. To enable the children to understand this personally I would like to ask each one, with your help, to plan a savings program for buying something he or she wants or a gift for someone else. Here are some of the things you can do:

1. Talk about whether the item your child has chosen is realistic, and if not, help choose another.

2. Help find out how much it would cost.

3. Ask how much your child already has to spend and help figure out how much more must be saved.

4. Think together about where the money will come from (allowances, earnings, etc.) and how much time it will take to save the amount needed.

5. Have your child make a plan for saving and help him or her follow the plan.

6. Make the final purchase a special occasion.

I hope this project will give you and your child lots of opportunity to talk about managing money. Happy planning!

Sincerely,

NAME _____

COUPON SHOPPING

My coupon was for _____

It was good for the following sizes: _____

I (did) (did not) find it on the shelf.

COST COMPARISON

BRAND	SIZE	WEIGHT OR VOLUME	COST

THE MONEY POT

DAY OF THE WEEK	AMOUNT IN THE POT	NUMBER OF TENS	AMOUNT ADDED
Monday			
Tuesday			
Wednesday			
Thursday			
Friday		--------	-------

PATTERNS

IN THE _____ FAMILY'S PHONE LIST

These numbers have repeated digits:

_____ _____ _____ _____

These numbers have all even digits:

_____ _____ _____ _____

These numbers have all odd digits:

_____ _____ _____ _____

These numbers have some digits which go up or down in order.

_____ _____ _____ _____

Here are some other patterns we found:

PATTERN   NUMBER

_____   _____

_____   _____

_____   _____

_____   _____

A BALANCE FOR WEIGHING MAIL

Using a pair of pliers, squeeze the ends of a coat hanger together and bend up.

Punch four holes just below the rim of an 8-ounce yogurt cup. Cut three 16-inch pieces of string.

Thread the ends of two of the pieces of string through opposite holes in the cup and tie, leaving equal length loops.

Put the third string through the hole in the spring of a clothespin and tie the ends together.

Hang the cup and the clothespin on the bent-up ends of the hanger.

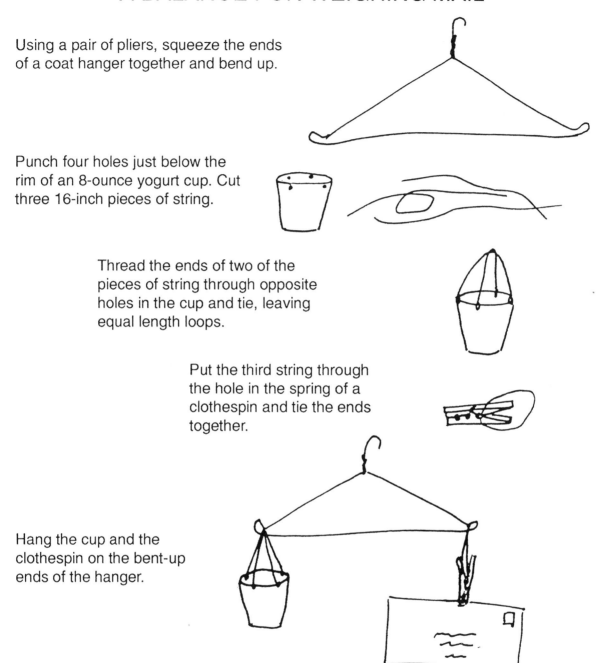

Find a place to hang the balance where it can swing freely on a nail or hook. Experiment with bending the curved top of the hanger until the ends come to rest at equal heights.

To use your balance, clip the mail on one side and place pennies in the cup until the ends of the hanger are balanced again. Each penny weighs about one tenth of an ounce (0.1 oz.). Count the pennies to find the weight of your letter.

THIS LETTER IS ABOUT LEARNING TO SORT AND CLASSIFY MAIL

Dear Parents,

Your children have probably been telling you about our classroom post office. They have worked hard to learn how to read a postal scale, how to weigh letters and figure out the right amount of postage, and how to make the correct change for their customers. The children have also learned how to order stamps from the post office. It would be great your child could be in charge of putting the correct postage on your outgoing mail. Since a postal scale would be helpful, I'm including directions for a simple homemade scale in case you don't have one.

This week, the students will make a mail survey in school: they will learn about different types of mail and will practice sorting it into separate categories and charting the results by number and weight.

Next week, your child will be asked to categorize your incoming mail for a period of two weeks. He or she will bring home a form for recording the results of this daily mail survey. Please allow your child to count and weigh the pieces of mail in each category, and if necessary, help in recording the results.

The children have been enjoying the post office activities and have learned a lot of math. Encourage them to tell you about it!

Sincerely,

FAMILY MAIL SURVEY

DATE: _____   NAME: _____

TYPE OF MAIL	NUMBER OF PIECES	WEIGHT

FAMILY MAIL SURVEY

DATE: _____   NAME: _____

TYPE OF MAIL	NUMBER OF PIECES	WEIGHT

NAME_____

TRAFFIC COUNT

Street _____ Town _____

Date I watched _____ Day of the Week _____

Time of Day_____ I watched for _____ minutes.

Here's what I saw:

CARS

VANS

TRUCKS

MOTORCYCLES

BICYCLES

THIS LETTER IS ABOUT KEEPING TRACK
OF YOUR CAR'S GAS CONSUMPTION

Dear Parents,

Have your children been talking about their most recent math study—calculating the rate of a car's gas consumption? In preparation for this assignment, we have been discussing the meaning of the term "miles per gallon": we have walked a mile, looked at gallon jugs and cans, and studied area maps to find familiar towns that are approximately thirty miles apart. The children are beginning to understand how much gas is used by a car that "gets" thirty miles per gallon (mpg).

We've practiced how to keep track of and calculate a car's mileage and gas consumption, and we've also talked about road and driving conditions that may influence gas consumption—in the city or on highways; on flat, hilly, paved, or gravel roads; in good or bad weather; in light or heavy traffic.

The children now need practice in a real situation and are looking forward to keeping track of their family car's rate of gas consumption. I've enclosed a chart for you to use for this purpose, as well as directions that outline the method the students used when making these calculations in school. I hope they will be able to practice with you and that everyone will enjoy this family project. Records like these can be most useful when you take longer family trips, and your children will gain valuable skills keeping these records.

Good luck!

NAME_____

GASOLINE CONSUMPTION

Date	Odometer Reading	Number of Miles Driven	Amount of Gas Used	Miles Per Gallon	Cost of One Gallon	Total Cost	Driving Conditions

HOW TO USE THE CHART ON GASOLINE CONSUMPTION

The first time you stop for gas, fill in only the first two columns of the chart—the date and the odometer reading. The next time you get gas, fill in all the columns.

Number of Miles Driven: The difference between the first and second odometer reading.

Amount of Gas Used: The amount of gas put into the tank on the second odometer reading.

Miles per Gallon: The number of miles you have driven your car using a gallon of gas. Divide the number of miles you drove by the amount of gas you used. For example, if you drove 265 miles and used 8 gallons of gas (i.e., 265 ÷ 8), your car got 33.125 miles per gallon.

Cost of One Gallon: Remember when that used to be under a dollar?!

Total Cost: The total cost for the gas you bought.

Driving Conditions: City streets; open highway; stop-and-go traffic; etc.

Also available from Heinemann. . .

Read Any Good Math Lately?
Children's Books for Mathematical Learning, K-6
David J. Whitin and **Sandra Wilde**

Mathematics has always had a story behind it. It is the story of measuring pigs, sharing cookies, calculating profits, weighing elephants, designing quilts, and cooking pancakes. It is through stories that learners come to view mathematics as a valuable tool, designed to pose questions and solve problems. Children's literature can be a powerful vehicle for sharing these stories with learners. Books provide an authentic context for mathematical use; they celebrate mathematics as a language for describing and framing our world; and they provide a non-threatening avenue for investigating a variety of mathematical concepts and relationships.

Read Any Good Math Lately? acquaints readers with some of the best children's books with a mathematical subtext: fiction, non-fiction, poetry, books of games and puzzles, books that reflect different cultures. The titles are diverse, but they all address a variety of mathematical topics: • place value • estimation • large numbers • geometry • measurement • fractions • classification • addition, subtraction, multiplication, and division. A comprehensive bibliography of books for all ages is provided for further exploration.

Full of children's work and numerous classroom scenarios, *Read Any Good Math Lately?* demonstrates the rich potential literature holds for engaging learners in a variety of mathematical investigations. It is an invitation to teachers, parents, and librarians to make the reading and sharing of good literature a natural part of mathematics teaching and learning.

1992   217pp   Paper

Heinemann
361 Hanover Street
Portsmouth, NH 03801-3912
(800) 541-2086